*'There are*
*where sou*
*Rome, Arc*
*to Ireland*
*without fi... Aran, and if people understood how greatly the Lord loves Aran they would all come there to partake of its blessings.'*

Cormac mac Cuilennáin,
King-Bishop of Cashel,died 908 AD.

*'The isles of Aran are famous for the numerous multitude of saints who lived and are buried there, or who trained in religious austerity and propagated monastic discipline in other parts; venerable for many sacred churches, chapels, wells, crosses, sepulchres, and other holy relics of saints still extant as monuments of their piety; reverenced for many rare privileges obtainable in the sacred places, and instant divine punishment inflicted on such as dare violate or profane them; frequently visited by Christians in pilgrimage for devotion, acts of penance, and the miracles wrought there.'*

Roderic O'Flaherty,
Description of West or H-Iar Connaught
1684 AD.

*'The Western Islands of Aran contain the greatest number of Pagan and early Christian monuments - military, domestic, ecclesiastical, and sepulchral - which can be found within the same area in Europe.'*

William Wilde, 1848 AD.

*'Baile Átha an Rí a bhí; Gaillimh atá; agus Árainn a bheas.'*
*'Athenry was; Galway is; and Aran will be.'*

Contemporary Saying.

An Chomhairle Oidhreachta — The Heritage Council

COMHAIRLE CHONTAE NA GAILLIMHE
GALWAY COUNTY COUNCIL

This publication has received support from the Heritage Council under the 1998 Publications Grant Scheme and from Galway County Council's Heritage Grant Scheme 2002.
Deontaisí faighte ón Chomhairle Oidhreachta agus Comhairle Chontae na Gaillimhe scéim deontaisí don oidhreacht 2002.

Aisling Árann

**December 1998**

**ISBN: 0 9534792 1 8**

**Revised and enlarged edition August 2002**

**(ISBN 0 9534792 0 X. 1st edition)**

Published by Aisling Árann, Árainn, Co. na Gaillimhe, Éire.
Tel.: +353-(0)99-61245. Fax: +353-(0)99-61968
E-mail: aismag@iol.ie

Illustrations: Gay McCarron, except where otherwise acknowledged.
Cover art: Tess Harper.
Editorial Assistance: Robert Allen, Tess Harper.
Typesetting, layout and design: Aisling Publications.
Printing: Clódóirí Lurgan, Indreabhán, Co. na Gaillimhe.

# POCKET GUIDE TO
# Árainn

Inis Mór, Aran Islands

# LEGENDS IN THE LANDSCAPE

**Dara Ó Maoildhia**

*Illustrated by Gay McCarron*

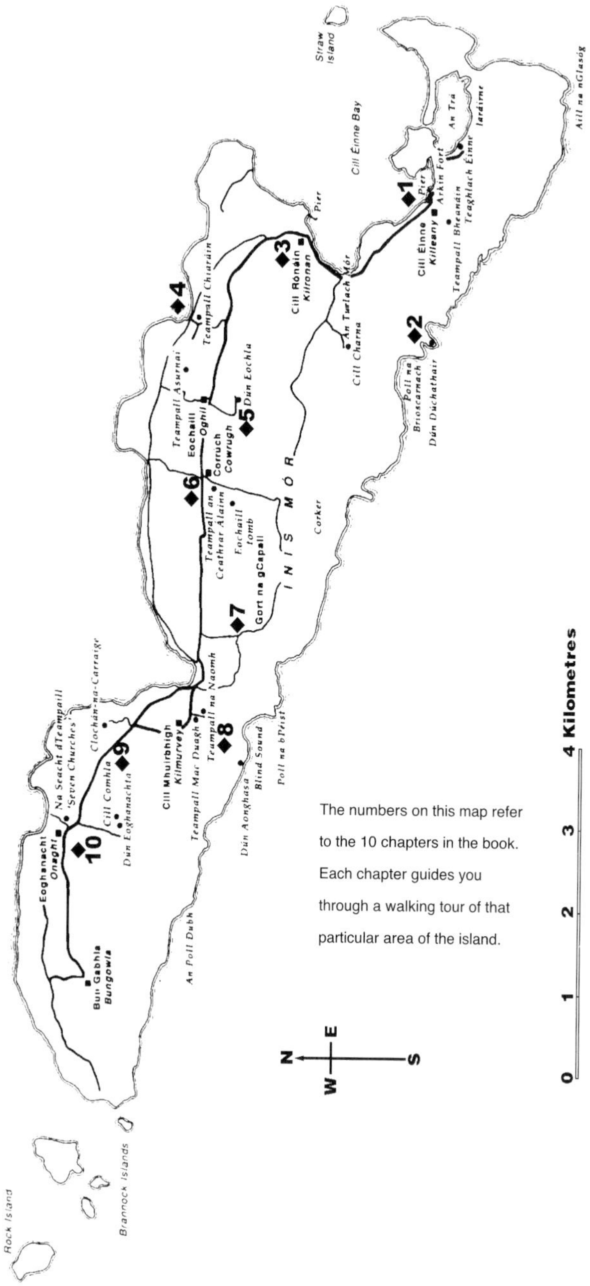


The numbers on this map refer to the 10 chapters in the book. Each chapter guides you through a walking tour of that particular area of the island.

# Inserts

# Cover Picture

*Manannán*, the Celtic God of the sea, is the son of Lir. Manannán guides souls to *Tír na n-Óg*, the land of youth. However, he is a master of tricks and illusions. He has the power to conceal islands in mist or even to make them disappear. His boat, *The Ocean Sweeper*, sails the seas without sail, rudder or oar. He also has a horse, *Aonbarr,* who can travel on land or sea alike, and a sword, *Fragarach,* which no armour can resist. Manannán wears a great cloak which is capable of taking on every kind of colour, just like the sea itself.

**I dedicate this book**

**to the people**

**who have added**

**wonderful colours**

**to my life:**

**Tess, Tuán, Macha and Surnaí.**

***Dara Ó Maoildhia*** is a priest in the Celtic tradition. His work includes leading pilgrimages and groups around Inis Mór. The present book is a fruit of this work. With his wife, Tess Harper, he edits and publishes The AISLING Magazine. They have three children.

# Introduction

I have lived on Inis Mór since January 1985. In that time, I have seen the number of visitors to the island increase from less than 10,000 a year to over 200,000 a year. Aran has become a Mecca for tourists and has achieved fame in TV documentaries, magazines and tourist books the world over. The great fort of Dún Aonghusa and the thousands of miles of stone walls have provided dramatic images that capture the imagination.

There is no doubt that Árainn (the correct name for Inis Mór) is a unique place. It has a richness far beyond the average tourist destination in its beauty, its archaeological heritage, and its local culture. Those who visit the island only briefly have little chance to experience the depth of this richness, but may taste enough to want to come back for more.

In ancient times there were no tourists but many travellers. Árainn was an important place to visit. At one stage it ranked next to Jerusalem and Rome as a place of pilgrimage, at least as far as the Irish monks were concerned.

This book is written not so much for the tourist as for the traveller. It is for those who, when they come to the island, want to engage with it and its people. It is for the quester, the searcher, the pilgrim, the spiritually hungry and those on a journey.

What you read here is what I have gathered and used for myself. It has given, and continues to give, nourishment to my soul. In more recent years, I have shared this knowledge with many individuals and groups who have visited the island. In that process it has become more clarified, accurate and complete. I offer it now to all those who are visiting presently, have visited in the past, or would like to visit in the future. My fervent hope is that it will touch and nourish your soul.

# 1

# Cill Éinne - *Killeany*

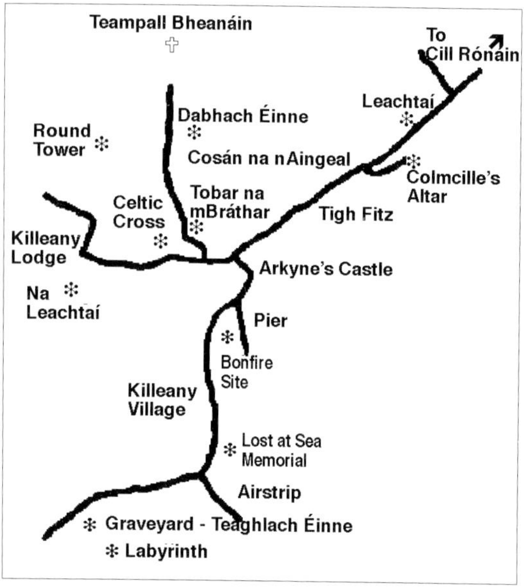


## *Teaghlach Éinne*

Teaghlach Éinne is a little church, half buried in the sand, in Killeany graveyard. You will find the graveyard at the far end of Cill Éinne (Killeany) village, past the airstrip. The graveyard is at least 1500 years old and is still in use as the main burial grounds of the island. It contains the grave of St Enda who died around 535 A.D. Before the road was built, funerals came here across the sand dunes and beach.

Step across the stile into the graveyard, walk the main path up through it and then bear left until you find the old church half buried in the sand. This is known as Teaghlach Éinne, literally the 'household' of Saint Enda. The notice tells you that Enda is buried here with 120 other saints. It is possible that Enda is buried under the altar, although others say he is buried to the north-east

## Enda of Aran

*Enda was a prince. His father's kingdom was Oriel on the North-East coast of Ireland (Louth-Monaghan). His sister Fanchea was baptised by St Patrick and subsequently became a consecrated virgin. Enda helped her build her monastery in a place now called Killanny in Monaghan. In the process he was converted by her.*

*He travelled Europe as a young monk seeking his "place of resurrection'. On his travels he was influenced by St Martin of Tours, St Honoratus on the Isle of Lerins, St David in Wales and St Ninian in Whithorn, Scotland. However, eventually he returned to Ireland and set up monasteries on the river Boyne near his home.*

*Enda's other sister Darina married the King of Cashel, Aonghus. They lived in a castle on the Rock of Cashel in Tipperary. Through the influence of his sister, Enda had an opportunity to build monasteries in the southern kingdom, which covered the southern half of Ireland, including Aran. Enda, to the king's surprise, requested Aran and was granted it. The request was granted through the intercession of St Ailbe of Emly, one of the four monastic bishops in Ireland before St Patrick. Enda came to Aran around 485 AD with 150 monks and set up ten monasteries across the island.*

*Teaghlach Éinne is the place of resurrection of Enda of Aran. He died around 535 AD. His body faces east to greet the rising Easter sun.*

*Teaghlach Éinne*

of the church.

Inside the church is an altar, some bullán stones and parts of a Celtic Cross. The altar has some carvings on it, and on its right side some writing. Notice how the spirals are drawn in both directions. The bullán stones look like holy-water fonts, but may also have been used for milling grain, or mixing dyes. The pillar made of parts of a Celtic Cross was cemented together in the 1980s as a way of preserving pieces. One piece belongs to the cross near the Round Tower (half a mile away). Some other bits were taken to the museum in Dublin. You can see on one of the pieces the carving of a horse and rider. This is likely to represent the time around the year 1000 AD when people thought the end of the world was nigh. The horse would represent the horse of the apocalypse.

***The 'Man of Aran'***

Before you leave the graveyard it is worth looking around at the gravestones. Most of them are inscribed in English. During the post-Cromwellian Penal Times (17th to 19th centuries) English was the official language and it was forbidden to speak Irish. Even though Irish survived in the homes, English was used in schools and in other public places. Close to Teaghlach Éinne as you face north-west you will find the tombstone of Tiger King who played the lead male role in the famous 1930s film 'The Man of Aran'.

### *Labyrinth*

Coming out of the graveyard, turn left and left again, walking towards the sea with the wall of the graveyard on your left. As you get close to the shore, you will notice a labyrinth laid out in stone in the field on your right. It was created by local people and is available for use. You are asked not to disturb lapwings that may be nesting in the grass nearby. The lapwing population is dangerously low and the species is now protected. You are also invited to add extra stones to the labyrinth where necessary.

### *Cill Éinne Village*

West towards Cill Rónáin (Kilronan) from the graveyard, you pass the airstrip on your right. Aer Árann was founded to service the three Aran Islands in 1970, largely through the inspiration and hard work of one islander, Colm Ó hIarnáin, or Colie Hernon. It is planned that a new terminal to be built here will be named after him.

Next you pass a memorial on your right which commemorates people lost at sea. It was erected in 1998. You will see, from the inscriptions on this memorial, how many young people have tragically died at sea, sometimes more than one from a single family. Many of the bodies have never been found.

The front face of the memorial commemorates a terrible tragedy that happened on August 15th 1852. Sixteen men from Cill Éinne village who were fishing off the Glasson Rocks were hit by a tidal wave. All of the men were drowned except one man. He was saved because his dog had drawn him away from the water's edge when the wave struck. In Roman Catholicism, August 15th is a holy day. It may be that the men were breaking church rules on that day, as all unnecessary work was forbidden on holy days. It is now a piseog (a superstitious practice) among traditional islanders not to fish off the Glasson Rocks on August 15th. (See also page 30).

A hundred yards further on, you will see a piece of waste

ground on the right with the obvious marks of a bonfire. This is the traditional bonfire site for Bonfire Night every year on St. John's Eve, June 23rd. On this night, each of the fourteen villages of the island gather around a bonfire which is lit at dusk and remains lighting until dawn. It is an opportunity for the whole village to come together to celebrate midsummer. The celebrations include the sharing of food and drink, music, singing and dancing.

Then you come to Cill Éinne Harbour. This was the original harbour for the whole island. To St Enda is attributed the miracle of carving out the channel through the rocks that lead to the pier. This channel is marked by stone pillars in the water. The harbour at Cill Rónáin was not developed until the 19th century, when it then replaced Cill Éinne as the main port.

***Arkyne's Castle***

Next to Cill Éinne Harbour is the remains of Arkyne's Castle. As the road comes to a sharp turn left at the harbour, directly ahead of you stands the turret of the castle and the remains of the sea wall. The road, which turns left and then right, gives you a good idea how big the castle was. It was built by the British Cromwellians in 1652-3.

The fort is known in Irish as Ballaí Chromwell (Cromwell's walls). It was built using the stones from Enda's church and the Franciscan friary, both located nearby. Up to two hundred men were garrisoned there. In 1657 it became a prison for priests and religious who were outlawed by the Penal Laws. Fifty or more priests were held there at one time.

The fort was garrisoned for thirty-three years and then was abandoned. The people of Cill Éinne then took the stones from the fort to build their homes. Although the Castle became a ruin in the late 1600s, British forces remained garrisoned on Aran in small numbers until the 1920s.

*Arkyne's Castle*

### *Tobar na mBráthar*

To get to Teampall Bheanáin (church of St Benan) take the signposted turn at a stone built house. As you enter the bóithrín (lane) a thatched chalet will be on your right. Past the chalet take a right turn onto a track. The first thing you meet here is the village well, no longer used but still in good condition with plenty of water. Further on up the track you will come across another well. This is known as Tobar na mBráthar, (the Well of the Friars).

The Franciscans came to Aran in the early 16th century and found that "in the islands of Aran of the Saints ... things of the church are neglected and there is ignorance of Christian doctrines". These were difficult times for them. Their Prior, Fr Gaspar Fonte, witnessed the demolition of his friary. He was subsequently imprisoned in Arkyne's Castle. Nonetheless, on and off, the Franciscans maintained a presence on Aran for nearly 200 years, up to 1697.

## The Monastic Village of Cill Éinne

*Standing at the Round Tower, cast your eye across the landscape below and imagine the great monastic village of Enda, stretching out in front of you, and as far to the right as Teaghlach Éinne in the distance. Unlike contemporary monastic structures, this monastery looked like a village. There were no large buildings. Monks lived in initially wooden huts, later stone huts called clocháns, in ones, twos or threes. Couples with children lived here also because the monastery needed artisans and workers of every kind. Students were also housed here. There were at least six churches that we know of scattered across the area. Monks prayed not only in the churches but also at the numerous Celtic crosses. These were painted in different colours, and a monk prayed there by walking around the cross — praying the rounds. The Round Tower provided a focus and centre point for the whole village. From its windows at the top, looking out in the four directions, the bells were rung to call people to prayer.*

...to page 17

... from page 16

*By creating this village, Enda offered a new model for living to people. Until now, people had only two choices - to live with their extended family or to marry into another. Now Enda was offering a new model - a monastic family that was created not through blood connections but through a common spiritual vision. Enda's monastery was revolutionary in Ireland. Soon the whole country was to be covered in monasteries like this one. For this reason, Enda is known as the patriarch of Irish monasticism.*

***Dabhach Éinne***

Further up this track you cross a stile and immediately before you is Dabhach Éinne, a covered well with a stone altar alongside. A dabhach is a barrel or casket. When St Enda first came to Aran he was confronted by the local chieftain Corban, who was not a Christian. Corban belonged to the Fir Bolg (bag men), a race of people who came to Ireland before the Tuatha de Danaan (the country people of the goddess Danu) and Celts, but who managed to survive, despite being a minority, into the Christian era. Corban required some proof of Enda's stature. It was agreed between them that a barrel of corn would be placed in the sea near Corcomroe in County Clare. If the barrel floated against the currents and the prevailing wind to Aran, then Enda would have proved his point. The barrel sailed to Aran directly, leaving a trail of perpetually calm water in its wake, to be seen to this day. It landed at Dabhach Éinne.

## The Fast of Enda and his Monks.

*When Enda, who was a son of the king of Oriel in County Louth, came to Aran he brought with him 150 monks and distributed them out across the island in ten different monasteries. A question arose as to whether Enda should be the abbot over all these monasteries, or whether they should have their independence. The issue was dealt with by doing a fast against God.*

*This may appear shocking, but St Patrick also fasted against God — for forty days on the top of Cruachán Aigle, now known as Croagh Patrick. In fact, fasting against God or against someone else (for example, hunger strikes) was such a common feature of Irish life that it had its own word in Irish to distinguish it from fasting 'for' something.*

*The Gaelic word for fasting 'against' is troscadh — still commonly used to denote the Lenten fast. The Gaelic word for fasting 'for' is aoin. Aoin gives its name to Dé hAoine (Friday) — the fast day. Céadaoin (Wednesday) — was the first day of fast in the week. Déardaoin( Thursday) — an Dé idir an dá aoin — was the day between the two fast days. Fasting 'for' was something you did on Wednesdays and Fridays. It meant having nothing to eat until late in the day (literally break-fast).*

*Enda and his monks continued to fast against God until one day an angel came from heaven to Enda with a book of the gospels and a cloak for his shoulders. The monks understood then that Enda was being given the cloak of authority to teach the gospels to them and they yielded to him.*

*Cross, Round Tower and Teampall Bheanáin*

### *Cosán na nAingeal*

In front of Dabhach Éinne and stretching west is a grassy creig (flat slab of rock), known as Cosán na nAingeal (the angels' footpath). Here Colmcille is said to have walked each day conversing with the angels. Angels were a big part of the monastic spirituality of the time, and each monastery and church had its own angels.

### *The Round Tower*

The Round Tower was initially thirty-five metres high. Its top was level with Teampall Bheanáin. During Cromwellian times it lost its two top stories, but remained twenty-five metres high. In the early nineteenth century it was hit by lightning, leaving only four metres. Round Towers were built across Ireland in the 9th and 10th centuries at the time of the Viking invasions. As well as look-outs, they were also bell-towers, places to store and exhibit relics and valuables, and places of refuge. A more recent theory assigns to them the same properties as a large oak tree, centring the energy of a place like an aerial and contributing to the fertility of the soil. There were many monasteries on Inis Mór but only one roundtower. The location of the roundtower at St Enda's monastery may therefore signify the primacy of this monastery over the others.

### *Celtic Cross*

Looking down to the east you will see the stub of a Celtic Cross in the middle of a field. It is now used as a scratching post for cattle! The cross, like all the other crosses on the island, was smashed by the Cromwellian troops. This was a deliberate act, to break the spirit of the people. A part of this cross is to be found in Teaghlach Éinne. Another part may indeed be a carved stone to be seen at low tide at Cill Éinne Pier below the wall of Arkyne's Castle. It lies among the rocks and sand, covered in seaweed. If you look carefully at the land close to the Celtic Cross you will see the contours of a building buried in the ground. This has never been archaeologically excavated, but one could surmise that here is the remains of St Enda's church.

### *Teampall Bheanáin*

At the top of the hill is the little church of St Benan. From here you will experience the panoramic view across both sides of the island, Inis Meáin, Inis Oírr to the south-east, and the Cliffs of Moher in Co. Clare to the east. Benan was a servant of St Patrick and became his successor in Armagh after he died. St Benan's church of course is not that old. It was probably built in the 11th century. There are very few stone churches that go back to the 5th century. It was only as the Celtic Church became established in the 8th century that long-lasting buildings made in stone were erected. Before that timber or clay and wattle were used.

The quality of masonry work on this church has stood the test of time in a very exposed place. It is a remarkably small church and was possibly used by a hermit associated with the monastery below. A few steps outside the door of the church is the remains of a clochán (beehive hut). This would suggest that the clochán was

*Teampall Bheanáin*

for sleeping and the church for praying. The hilltop position facilitated astronomical observation in which the Celtic monks had always held an interest. The church is unusual because it is not orientated east-west - the normal position. Instead it is northeast-southwest. This may have been to afford better shelter from the weather.

Across to the west at the same level as Teampall Bheanáin is the remains of a rectangular building called The Priest's House. This may be connected with a time after the 12th century when Celtic monasticism had died out and was replaced by religious orders from overseas. A Celtic monastery would not have had a priest's house, u't religious orders such as the Augustinians did have dormitory buildings for their priests. You will see another example of these dormitory buildings in Na Seacht dTempaill.

***Killeany Lodge***

Looking down from Teampall Bheanáin to the south, you will see an L-shaped house on its own, far removed from all the other houses down below nearer the sea. This house was known as the Hill Farm and was owned first by the Fitzpatrick's, who took possession of this part of the island in 1713. From here, the Fitzpatrick's were masters of all they surveyed, collecting rent from all who lived below them at the bottom of the hill. The bulk of the population of Inis Mór lived in Cill Éinne at this time, where the one good harbour provided shelter for their boats.

*Na Leachtaí - Stone Memorials*

In 1744, the Digby's took possession of the whole island. They put their bailiffs into Killeany Lodge and leased the western half of the island to a tenant farmer called O'Flaherty. He lived in a large stone house at Cill Mhuirbhigh (Kilmurvey), near Dún Aonghusa (Dun Aengus). This remained the situation until 1921 when the island was compulsorily purchased by the Congested Districts Board (later to become the Land Commission), a government agency that was conducting land reform. From then on islanders were able to purchase their own properties and no longer had to pay rents to landlords.

***Na Leachtaí - Stone Memorials***

Beyond Cill Éinne Lodge at its boundary wall are two clearly visible pillars, and one smaller, not so visible, pillar. These are memorials, or cenotaphs, built by the Fitzpatricks. The nearest commemorates three Fitzpatricks who died in quick succession: Dennis aged 23, John, 25 and Peter, 17. They all died between December 1753 and March 1754. Local people said it was typhus.

On the other memorial, John and Sara Fitzpatrick are commemorated. Their deaths occurred in February 1709 and November 1709 respectively. They were husband and wife, but too long dead to be the parents of the three boys. Monuments like these are to be found in various

## Enda and Colmcille

*When a prospective monk came to the island, Enda's practice was to welcome the visitor and to offer him or her a piece of land on which to build a cell. Many future Irish saints and founders came to Aran, some of them staying for a number of years before moving on. However, when the young Colmcille arrived, Enda refused to give him a piece of land.*

*Colmcille asked Enda for a piece of land the size of his cloak. He threw his cloak on the ground to illustrate. However, the cloak began to expand until it covered a whole field. At that point, Enda in a burst of anger grabbed up the cloak and threw it back at Colmcille. Colmcille was then banished from the island.*

*Behind the story lies some Irish politics that makes good sense. Enda was a prince of Oriel, a fairly minor northern kingdom. However, Colmcille was a prince of the northern O'Neill and could have been in the running for the high-kingship of Tara. That meant he was more powerful than Enda. "If I give you a piece of land," Enda told Colmcille, "this island will be remembered for you and not me".*

*Enda was probably correct about that! Even as it stands, Colmcille's day on June 9th is better remembered and celebrated by the people of Aran than Enda's day on March 21st.*

...to page 24

... from page 23

*The place where Colmcille's cloak expanded is known to this day as Gort na gCochall, (the field of the cloak). If you stand at Colmcille's Altar facing the sea, the field is on your left. Below you is where Colmcille fell when Enda pushed him. You can see the marks of Colmcille's ribs on the rocks.*

*To add insult to injury, Enda would not allow any of his monks to ferry Colmcille back to the mainland. The result was that Colmcille sat on a rock which turned into a boat. It lies precariously balanced on the rocks near the end of the airstrip and is best seen from a boat. The rock/boat is called 'Bád na Naoimh' (the Saint's Boat).*

*Not to be outdone, Colmcille put three curses on Inis Mór as he left it. The first curse was that the island would have no soil. Soil on the island has had to be created by islanders out of seaweed and sand. The second was that the island would have no fuel of its own — no turf. The third was that the island would always be ruled by outsiders.*

*These three curses can only be reversed by a saint greater than Colmcille — a tall order, as Colmcille was probably the greatest saint the Celtic Church ever had!*

*Altóir Colmcille*

parts of the island. Nowhere else in the country is there anything quite like it. They continued to be built up to the end of the 19th century, mostly along the side of the road, where people passing would be reminded to say a prayer for them.

### *Altóir Colmcille*

Heading towards Cill Rónáin on the main road, past the pub Tí Fitz on your right, you will discover a lane on the right leading down to the sea. Walk along the shore line towards Cill Rónáin across the dúirling (rounded stones). Be careful of your ankles and watch the slippy seaweed. At the end of the dúirling is an altar dedicated to St Colmcille. His name is carved at the base of the stone cross erected on the altar.

Traditionally people visit Altóir Colmcille on his feastday June 9th. People will arrive at any time of the day and do the rounds at the altar. Doing the rounds means walking in a sunwise (clockwise) direction around the altar seven times. You take seven pebbles in your hand before you begin and use these for counting your rounds. As you pass around each time you drop a stone at the altar.

This ritual is called a turas deiseal (a journey to the right). It originated with the Celts who did the ritual in imitation of the sun going round the earth. A journey to the right blesses and a journey to the left curses. In some parts of Ireland there are cursing stones. With a cursing stone, you turn it to the left to curse someone. The turas deiseal

### *Colmcille's Farewell to Aran*

*Farewell from me to Aran, a sad farewell I think;*
*I must go east to Iona, separated since the Flood.*
*A farewell from me to Aran; it torments my heart not to be*
*In the west by her billows, among throngs of heaven's saints.*
*A farewell from me to Aran, a sad farewell it is;*
*Aran full of fair angels; not even a servant with me in my currach.*
*The Son of God, oh it is the Son of God who sends me to Iona*
*And gives Enda (what prosperity!) Aran, the Rome of pilgrims.*
*Aran, Sun, oh Aran, Sun! my love stays with her in the west.*
*Whoever lies under her pure earth will never be seen by the devil's eye.*
*Saintly Aran, oh saintly Aran! Woe to him who is her foe,*
*For angels come from heaven to visit her every day of the week.*
*Gabriel comes each Sunday, for Christ has so ordered,*
*And fifty angels (no feeble power!) to bless her Masses.*
*Every Monday, oh every Monday, Michael comes (a great advantage)*
*And thirty angels (their habit is good) to bless her churches.*

... to page 27

... from page 26

*Every Tuesday, oh every Tuesday, Raphael comes, of mysterious power,*
*To bless the houses serving her guests.*
*On hard Wednesday, oh hard Wednesday, Urial comes (a great advantage),*
*And three times blesses her high angelic cemeteries.*
*On every Thursday, oh every Thursday, Sarial comes (a great treasure),*
*That God's beneficence be poured from heaven onto her bare stones that day.*
*On Friday, oh on Friday, comes Ramiel and his host,*
*That every eye be filled with the sight of truly bright beauteous angels.*
*Mary, Mother of God's Son, and her train comes too with angels among the host,*
*To bless Aran on a Saturday.*
*If there were no life in Aran but listening to her angels,*
*It would be bettter than any other life under heaven, to hear their celebrations.*

This version is thanks to
Tim Robinson in *Stones of Aran*

was Christianised by adding certain prayers as one did the rounds. The traditional prayers on Aran are the Ár nAthair (Our Father), Sé do bheatha, a Mhuire (Hail Mary), Glóir don Athair (Glory Be to the Father), and Cré na nAspal (the Apostles' Creed) (see page 96).

# 2
# Iar Áirne

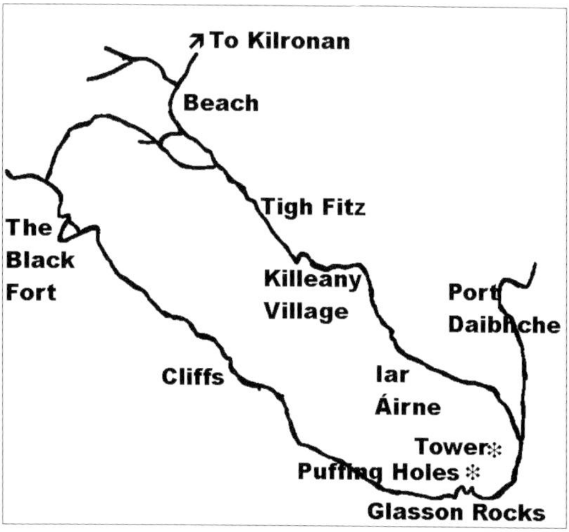


*Sketch of circuit*

Dún Dubhchathair (the Black Fort) can be visited on its own or as part of a circular walk around the south-eastern end of the island known as Iar Áirne. From Cill Rónáin, walking, allow 4 - 5 hours for the full circuit. On the cliff side, the going is very rough so wear good walking shoes or boots. A visit to Dún Dubhchathair on its own, from Cill Rónáin, walking, will take 2-3 hours.

***Dún Dubhchathair - The Black Fort***

From Cill Rónáin, head towards Cill Éinne about one mile as far as the disused electricity generation station on the right hand side. It is a grey building tucked in under a cliff with a small salt lake beside it. Take the turn to the right here. At the top of the hill turn right again and follow the road out to the cliffs.

On the right you will pass a turlough (a lake that dries up). There are large concrete storage tanks on the far side of the turlough. This is where the island gets its water. New and larger water storage tanks have been

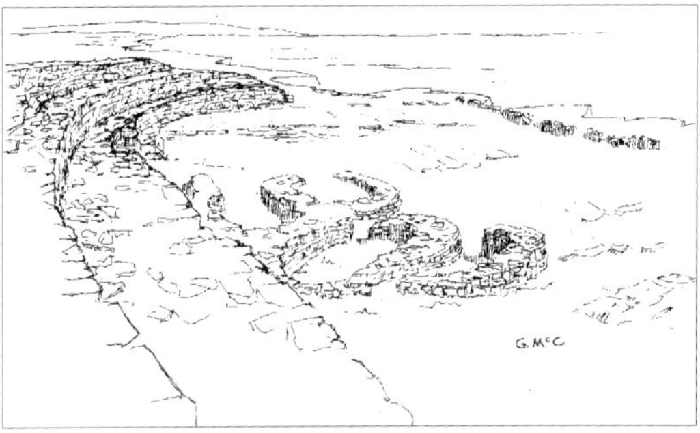


*Dún Dubhchathair - The Black Fort*

built further up the hill below Dún Eochla. The water is pumped from the smaller tanks to the bigger ones, and this ensures a continuous water supply for the island.

The small storage tanks are in an area called Carna where there are the remains of a monastic church and clocháns and a holy well. In the 1800's people who were suffering from an epidemic were sent here to live and perhaps die, away from the general population.

As the road begins to rise, cast your eye to the right to the rock face on the far side. If you are visiting during Spring or early Summer, you will spot a large number of herons nesting in the bushes and on the cliff face. Heron's nest as a colony and this area is the island's heronry. Please be careful not to disturb them.

The road deteriorates towards the cliffs and eventually disappears altogether. When at the cliff face, take a left and Dún Dubhchathair will be before you.

Dún Dubhchathair is one of two cliff forts on Inis Mór, the other being Dún Aonghusa. It has a different 'feel' to it than Dún Aonghusa, not quite as spectacular - but some people prefer it. Inside the stone wall enclosure are the remains of clocháns that were used as dwellings. There is also a tunnel under a wall which possibly was an escape route to the outside. Outside the wall is the remains of *Chevaux de Frise*, large stones set at differing angles in the ground. These were placed to make it difficult for attackers. You will see a better example of this at Dún Aonghusa (see page 72).

Whether people lived here permanently or simply in times of danger is not known. There is no well or water source nearby, and it is in an exposed and barren spot. As with Dún Aonghusa, this fort is likely to have been used for celebratory purposes as well as for temporary refuge.

Parts of the cliff around the fort have been eroded and the fort itself is slowly falling into the sea. In the 1800s the fort was a broken down ruin. It was rebuilt in 1880. Its present outline may not be true to the original. The buttresses on the outside were added at this time.

### *The Glasson Rocks*

From Dún Dubhchathair it is about an hour's walk over a rough rock surface to The Glasson Rocks. These rocks are at the end of the island and face southwest. The cliff-face drops down to a platform of flat rock just above sea-level.

Islanders traditionally fish from here using lines and rods and can catch *ballach* (rockfish), *mangach* (pollock) and *ronnach* (mackerel). It is a difficult climb down onto these rocks and is dangerous in rough weather as waves can wash across the platform.

On August 15th 1852 fifteen men were drowned here while fishing when a tidal wave swept over them. As August 15th was a holyday, the Feast of the Assumption, the men (according to their religion) should not have been working. The accident was attributed to God's anger and no islander fishes off the Glasson Rocks on August 15th since then. A memorial to these and others lost at sea was erected in Cill Éinne village and unveiled on August 15th 1998. (See also page 13).

### *Gleann na nDeor*

Near the Glasson Rocks is the place where islanders gathered in the 1800s to see the boats from Galway

## Inis Mór Mens' Christian Names

***Éanna - Enda:*** *St Enda was the first Christian monk to come to Aran. He founded his monastery at Cill Éinne in the late 5th century. Feastday March 21.*
***Colman:*** *St Colman Mac Duach studied with St Enda on Inis Mór. Teampall Mac Duach is in the grounds of Kilmurvey House. From Inis Mór he moved to County Clare where he founded the monastery of Kilmacduagh, later to become a diocese. Feastday October 29.*
***Máirtín - Martin:*** *St Martin of Tours founded a community outside Tours in France in the late 4th century. Many Irish monks came to visit him there. St Martin's feastday is Nov. 11th. Traditionally, animals and fowl are killed on this day.*
***Macdara - Dara:*** *St Macdara's island lies off Litir Ciaráin in Connemara and can been seen from Inis Mór. Macdara built his hermitage there in the 6th century and lived alone. His feastday is July 16th.*
***Colm - Coley:*** *St Colmcille or Columba is one of the greatest of the Irish monastic saints. He was a prince of the O'Neill's of Ulster. He came to Aran as a young monk. Altóir Colmcille is in Cill Éinne and marks the spot where he came ashore. Islanders traditionally visit this shrine on his feastday, June 9th.*
***Ciarán:*** *St Ciarán, founder of the great monastery at Clonmacnoise, came to Aran as a young monk. His hermitage on Aran grew into a famous monastery called Mainistir Connacht. That part of Inis Mór is now known simply as Mainistir. His feastday is Sept.9th.*
***Gregory:*** *Pope St Gregory of the Golden Mouth died in Rome but his body was put in a casket and dropped into the river Tiber. It landed on Aran at Port Daibhche, Iar Áirne. The saint's body was buried under Martin's Tower, overlooking Inis Meáin. The gap between the two islands is known as Gregory's Sound. Boats traditionally dipped their sails out of respect for St Gregory on passing through.*
***Caomhán - Kevin:*** *St Caomhán is associated with Inis Oírr and is said to be the brother of St Kevin of Glendalough. A church half-buried in the sand commemorates him on Inis Oírr. His burial site near the church is the most sacred spot on the island.*

sailing for America filled with emigrants. The little valley close to the Glasson Rocks is called Gleann na nDeor (the vale of tears).

### *The Puffing Holes*

Beside the Glasson Rocks are some spectacular caves. Three of them emerge as blow-holes on the surface of the cliff. The biggest and most spectacular one is 100 feet back from the cliff edge and is 40 feet in diameter. Two other less spectacular blow holes are to be found further back from the cliff.

All along the cliff edge is a gathering of loose rocks, known as a storm beach. These rocks have been washed up onto the top of the cliff and then pushed back as if some great god of the sea had used a giant sweeping brush. When the seas are rough and the wind is blowing a gale from the west, the cliffs of Inis Mór are dangerous for an inexperienced visitor.

### *St Gregory's Sound*

Heading on from the Glasson Rocks around the southern tip of Inis Mór, Inis Meán is a stone's throw away across St Gregory's Sound. The St Gregory referred to here is Pope Gregory of the Golden Mouth. He died in Rome but his body was placed in a casket on the river Tiber and it sailed to Aran. It landed at Port Daibhche (the Port of the Cask), the next beach along the coastline. Gregory is buried beneath Túr Máirtín (Martin's Tower), a tower to be seen at the top of the hill overlooking the sound. Traditionally, ships passing here dipped their sails in honour of Gregory.

Túr Máirtín was probably built as a look-out tower, and got its name from a Máirtín who once owned the land.

Once past the hill of Túr Máirtín, a track to the left brings you away from the water's edge and back towards Iar Áirne. After a short trek through a rabbit-inhabited field you cross a wall and rediscover the road that will lead you back through Cill Éinne and on to Cill Rónáin again.

# 3
# Cill Rónáin

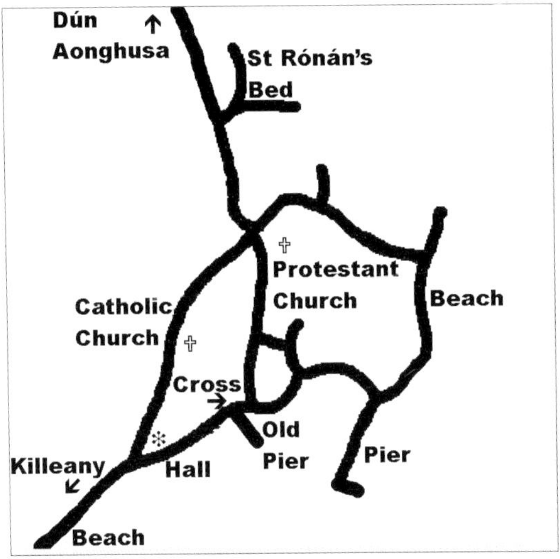


In 1812, there were 52 houses in Cill Rónáin and 78 in Cill Éinne. At that time, Cill Éinne was the main population centre of Inis Mór and had been since the time of Enda in the 6th century.

### *Kilronan Pier*

The key moment in the growth of Cill Rónáin was the building of the new pier in 1853, shortly after the Famine. The Protestant church was also built around this time (1846). Add to this the rectory, the constabulary barracks and the coastguard station and you can see how Cill Rónáin became the capital of the Aran Islands. It is now the main village of Inis Mór with about 200 inhabitants.

### *The Celtic Cross*

In the centre of the village, overlooking the harbour, is a fine Celtic cross, a memorial to Fr Michael O'Donoghue, Catholic parish priest from 1881 to 1892. Fr O'Donoghue came to Aran at a time when famine was again threatening. He is famed for sending a telegram to Dublin

Castle in 1886 with the words: SEND US BOATS OR SEND US COFFINS.

By the end of the 1890s, life for the islanders had improved enormously. Six national schools were now in operation. Rents had been reduced and tenants given some legal protection. A telegraph office (morse code) had been opened on the island. A cargo vessel was sailing three times a week from Galway. The fishing fleet had grown and was having great success.

Fr O'Donoghue had been a tireless worker on behalf of the islanders, and they celebrated his memory with this fine memorial in his honour. The cross was carved by James Pearse of Dublin, father of Patrick Pearse, a leader of the 1916 uprising.

### *Halla Rónáin*

Turning right at the cross and heading towards Cill Éinne, Halla Rónáin is about 200 yards away overlooking the sea. This hall was built in 1966 and has been added to and refurbished substantially since then. It now houses a modern gymnasium, a youth club room, café area and large dance hall. Across the road from the hall are the Health Board buildings where the doctor and nurse reside and hold their clinics.

### *The Catholic Parish Church*

Turning up this road at the back of the hall, you arrive at the Catholic Church of St Brigid. Built in 1905, it superceded the church in Eochaill as the main parish church. The church was modernised in the late seventies by the parish est Fr Tadhg Ó Móráin. He removed the balcony, exposed the stone on the inside walls,

*The Protestant Church of St Thomas (Church of Ireland)*

modernised the sanctuary, replaced the confessionals with a confession parlour, and replaced the traditional statues and stations of the cross with more modern creations. Outside the church is a statue of St Brigid, placed there in 1994 by the local health nurse, Clára Ní Ghiolla. Some oak trees were also planted in the grounds of the church at this time to honour St Brigid.

### *The Protestant Church*

The Protestant church of St Thomas (Church of Ireland) is at the top of the hill on the main road overlooking Kilronan. It was built to serve the Church of Ireland population that had been posted to the island. The islanders themselves of course were all Catholic. The church is now roofless, having fallen into disuse after the Free State was declared in 1922. The rectory, now demolished, was located among the fine glen of trees, to the west of the church, called Garraí na Dóibe (the daub garden — dóib is a type of clay like putty, found here and used for plastering).

Facing downhill towards Cill Rónáin, the coastguard station is immediately on the left, the constabulary barracks on the right. The coastguard station is now divided up between the Gardaí, Telecom Éireann, the Library and the Heritage Centre. The latter houses the local community co-operative Comharchumann Forbartha Árann. The barracks building is now shared between a pub, the Post Office and a craft shop.

***Leaba Naomh Rónáin***

Heading out of Cill Rónáin uphill along the main road towards Dun Aonghusa, a pub called Joe Watty's marks a turn to the right. Following this road to where it swings left again, we come across an old ruin dedicated to St Rónán who has given his name to the village. This place is known as An Atharla, the burial place. Rónán is buried here and the little chapel is to his memory. As in many other places, the tradition was to lie on his grave overnight on the eve of his feastday (August 15th) and seek a cure to whatever ailment bedevilled you.

While most of the other saints remembered on the island are identifiable, St Rónán is an unknown. No stories remain about him. It may be that he is the same Rónán that is celebrated with great festivities in Lacronan, Brittany. This Rónán lived in the 7th century and his feastday is June 1st. It was Irish and Welsh monks who brought the Celtic form of Christianity and the Celtic language to Brittany. The connection remains to this day through the Pan-Celtic Festival and other such events.

This road will bring you to the next village, Mainistir.

# 4
# Mainistir

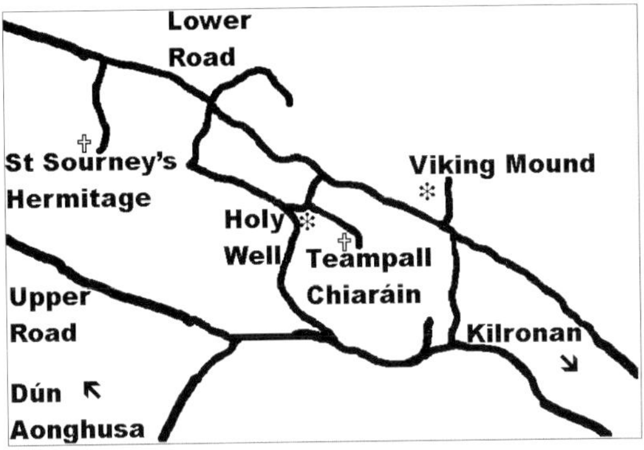


From Cill Rónáin, take the turn right at Joe Watty's Pub and follow An Bóthar Ó Thuaidh (Lower Road) with the sea on your right.

As you approach the camping site, a plaque on the wall on the left marks the spot where a local man was shot and killed by the Black and Tans in 1920. His name was Larry Beag, or Laurence McDonagh, and he was trying to get to Mass on Sunday, creeping behind the walls to avoid being seen.

### *Viking Burial Mound*

Past the camping site on the right hand side is a mound, which on close inspection is clearly manmade. It is a burial mound. On the top is a cross-inscribed standing stone. The mound overlooks the sea and has the shape of a large, upturned boat. A likely explanation is that it was built to bury a Viking chieftain. The Viking practice was to bury the chieftain under his upturned boat and then cover the whole lot with stones and soil. Vikings attacked Ireland and especially its monasteries from the 9th to the 11th centuries. The last known attack on Aran was in 1081.

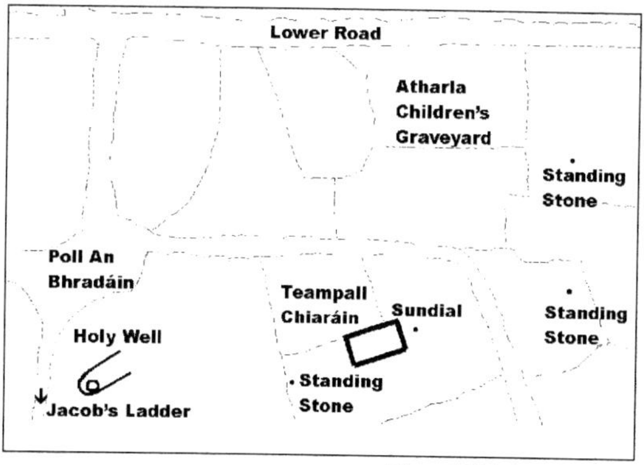


*Plan of Mainistir Chiaráin*

### *Mainistir Chiaráin*

Mainistir Chiaráin can be approached from the Lower Road at Port Mhainistir or from the Upper Road at a fork to the right past Mainistir Hostel. It incorporates a number of different sites, which we will visit in turn.

### *Poll an Bhradáin*

Approaching Teampall Chiaráin from either direction, you will come across a concrete water tank. It is worth stopping here for a minute. This is Poll an Bhradáin, the Salmon Pool. According to legend, when St Enda first arrived on Aran, he landed here. He had 150 monks with him and no food. By the third day they were very hungry. Miraculously, a large salmon appeared in the pool and was big enough to feed all of them.

This story connects with the Celtic myth 'The Salmon of Knowledge'. In this story, Fionn McCumhail tastes the otherworld salmon which has been caught by Finegas the poet on the River Boyne. In doing so he receives all the knowledge that the salmon had consumed when it ate the hazel nuts hanging out over the source of the sacred river.

For the Greeks, the secret sign of a Christian was the fish — ICHTHUS. The letters stood for 'Jesus Christ God and Man'. For the Celts, that fish is An Bhradán Feasa (the Salmon of Knowledge).

### *Jacob's Ladder*

Close to the water tank is a narrow steep footpath leading up to the next terrace. This is known as Jacob's Ladder — a name probably given to it by the monks who lived here. This name refers to a Biblical story (Genesis 28:10-22) in which Jacob had a dream. He saw a ladder on which angels were ascending and descending between earth and heaven. When he awoke he acknowledged that this place was indeed the gate of heaven.

### *Holy Well of St Ciarán*

In the small field to the left of Jacob's Ladder and directly above Poll an Bhradáin is the Holy Well of St Ciarán. This is visited by locals on September 9th, the feast of St Ciarán. In earlier times there was a passageway up from Poll an Bhradáin directly to this well. You can imagine the people of the village gathering at the lower well to collect their daily water supply and visiting the upper holy well to make the rounds and say their prayers.

Making the rounds is called a turas deiseal (a journey to the right), and is done by taking seven pebbles in one's hand and doing seven rounds of the well in a clockwise direction, using the pebbles as counters. The pebbles are available in a stone basin near the well. You drop a stone each time you pass the stone basin. Traditionally, the common prayers — Our Father, Hail Mary, Creed (see page 96) — are recited. On completion of the seven rounds you approach the well and reach into the water for a drink, a blessing, or to fill a bottle for taking away.

### *The Church Building*

Teampall Chiaráin is a large building by Aran standards. When Ciarán came here at the beginning of the 6th century, he would have built a more modest structure, probably with timber or clay and wattles. Stone buildings emerged a few centuries later when the Celtic Church became more established.

Nonetheless, this building has been around for a long time. The west gable door is possibly as early as the 8th

## The Holy Well
## An Tobar Bheannaithe

*In Celtic mythology, a well is sacred because it is an entrance into the womb of Mother Earth, the goddess Danu or Bríd. Ireland inherited its Christian holy wells, and the practice of doing the rounds, from this ancient heritage.*

*At a deep level, wells are healing, life-giving places that can reconnect us with our earth mother, with the sun and the seasons, and with our own biological rhythms.*

*Wells are symbols of the feminine, representing sexuality, fertility, menstrual cycles, and the earth's fruitfulness. Reaching deep down into the well, we can find healing for related ills.*

*Wells are associated with healing for the eyes. A well looks like an eye, and we can see our reflection in it.*

*If you see bubbles of air in a well, this is a sign that you will receive inspiration. If you see a little fish in a well, this is a sign that you will receive wisdom or knowledge.*

*A round of the well is done by walking in a clockwise direction, imitating the sun. On Aran usually seven rounds are done, counting with small pebbles collected near the well and dropped back each time one passes. Pray as you go. On completion of the rounds, go to the well and take some water.*

*cf. An Turas Deiseal page 42.*

*Teampall Chiaráin*

century. The east gable window is 12th century and the north facing door is medieval 16th century. This gives the present building a span of 900 years. The monastic presence on the site was probably 1100 years.

The window and two doors mark very important moments in Irish church history. The 8th century represents the zenith of Irish monasticism, when Ireland earned its title "The Island of Saints and Scholars". The peace dividend of this time brought about a flourishing of scholarship and of arts and crafts and revolutionised Irish society. It is during this time that such works as the Book of Kells, the Ardagh Chalice and the great stone Celtic Crosses were created. This Golden Age was shattered a century later by the attacks of the Vikings.

The 12th century represents the time when the Celtic Church lost its power to a more Roman model of church. On the political front, Henry II had successfully invaded Ireland at the behest of the Pope. On the ecclesiastical front, the same Pope at last got a firm hold on Ireland by replacing the power of the monasteries and their abbots with his bishops and priests. St Malachy of Armagh was the leader of this transformation and became the first archbishop of Armagh. During the 12th century, Ireland was colonised politically by Britain and ecclesiastically by Rome.

## The Rounds - An Turas Deiseal

*The rounds is a traditional Celtic spiritual practice that originated in pre-Christian times and was practiced also by the early Celtic monks. It is still common all over Ireland and is done around holy wells, graves, churches and crosses.*

*When the Celts —or Milesians as they are also known — first invaded Ireland, they sailed around the island three times before finding a place to land. To the Celts, the land of Ireland was the sacred Goddess. They were wedded to the land through their kings, whose coronation ceremonies were wedding rituals.*

*The land of Ireland is a woman whose breasts are in Kerry (two mountains called The Paps of Danu), her umbilical cord is at the hill of Uisneach in County Westmeath, the rivers and streams are her veins, and every well is an entrance to her womb.*

*In the northern hemisphere, the sun is perceived as travelling across the sky in a southerly arc. The turas deiseal imitates this on the ground. Going around the well clockwise, you are imitating the sun going around the earth. The male sungod unites with the earth goddess through her fertile womb-entrance — the well.*

*This ritual maintains humans in right relationship with the sun and the earth, and attunes them to the fertility cycles and to the seasons. Today, humankind has lost this right relationship with the earth and is out of touch with cycles and seasons. The practice of this ritual is now more important than ever.*

The 16th century marks the time of the Reformation and great upheaval in the church. This effected Ireland with the dissolution of the monasteries throughout the British Isles and later by the Cromwellian invasion. From this time on, there is no evidence of monastic activity on Aran. In fact, no religious order of any kind has established itself on Aran since then up to the present time, despite their proliferation throughout the rest of the country.

***Standing Stones***

Outside the west gable of Teampall Chiaráin there is a fine example of a standing stone. It has a cross inscribed on it and represents an early expression of a tradition that led to the great stone Celtic crosses. This standing stone may initially have been used on the island by pre-Christain Celts to mark a sacred place.

This Celtic practice was adapted by the monks and they used these stones to mark the boundaries of their monasteries, inscribing the stones with crosses and other symbols. Celtic monasteries were sanctuaries for those being pursued, for whatever reason. Boundary lines became very important in this context. The wanted person was safe within the boundary.

At the east gable outside the church is another standing stone. This is strictly a sundial. The hole at the top is designed to allow a stick to protrude. When the sun catches the stick, it throws a shadow on the dial below and indicates the time. The exact times of prayer may have been painted onto the dial in times past but are long since gone. The sundial is not in its original position, as to catch the sun its face should be turned south.

This sundial has been used in recent times as a wishing stone. A silk scarf is drawn through the hole three times while a wish is made. This ritual is particularly suited to someone seeking to have a child.

In earlier times, the sundial was used also as a contract

## St Ciarán

*St Ciarán came to Aran as a young monk to study under Enda. His father was a chariot maker from the North and his mother was from Kerry, but he was born in Connacht.*

*Ciarán lived on Aran for seven years. His work was threshing and grinding the corn for food and thatch. The church of St Ciarán was probably thatched.*

*While on Aran, Ciarán had a dream. He saw a large tree growing in the centre of Ireland. The birds were carrying its fruit all over the country. He told his dream to Enda who interpreted it. Ciarán was that tree and he was to build his monastery at Clonmacnoise on the banks of the Shannon. True to the dream, the monastery became one of the greatest monasteries in Ireland.*

*When Ciarán departed from Aran, Enda went to see him off and wept for the loss of a dear friend. He noticed that many of the angels of Aran went with him and this left him even more sorrowful. In his depression, Enda resorted to fasting against God until God consoled him with three promises: 1) all who died on Aran would go to heaven; 2) people would call on Enda in time of trouble; 3) Enda would sit closer to God's right hand on the day of judgement.*

*Ciarán died from the plague in 545 at the age of 33, just seven months after completing the building of his monastery. His feastday is September 9th.*

Sundial

stone. When people were illiterate and had no lawyers or solicitors to draw up contracts for them, contracts were sealed at this stone by both contractees touching fingers through the hole in the presence of witnesses. This ritual is an attractive one for couples making or renewing their marriage vows.

The making of the rounds is another ritual performed here. Walk in a clockwise direction around the sundial a number of times. Then make your wish as you put a scarf or hankerchief through the hole.

Standing with your back to the east gable at the sundial, you will see two other standing stones in fields nearby. On close inspection they are not only cross inscribed, but have little ears and a cap sculpted into them. They represent an early stage of the development of the full Celtic Cross and are quite unique.

***Reilig na Leanaí***

In a little graveyard, between the Teampall and the sea, you will find the broken remains of more of these crosses. This graveyard is Reilig na Leanaí (the children's graveyard) and was used to bury unbaptised children whose souls were believed to go to Limbo, a nondescript place between heaven and hell. Older children and at least one adult are also buried here. Older islanders remember infants being buried here in the dark of night without priest or ceremony. The practice has now been discontinued.

*St Sourney's Hermitage*

### *Augustine and Pelagius*

The theology behind this practice was the result of a victory of St Augustine over Pelagius. Pelagius was a Celtic monk who taught that we are born sinless and can only sin by an act of the will. He went to Rome and other major Christian centres in Europe to confront the emerging teaching of Augustine. Augustine was teaching that we are born with Original Sin. The only way we can be saved is to be baptised within the Church. The teaching of Pelagius represented Celtic Christian thought at the time. Although he was condemned and his teaching held to be anathema, Celtic Christianity remained 'Pelagian' for many centuries after his death.

### *Naomh Surnaí – St Sourney's Hermitage*

Travelling west along the Lower Road from Mainistir Chiaráin, a signpost on the left indicates a track through the fields to St Sourney's Hermitage — an excellent spot for contemplation.

St Sourney is the only woman saint remembered on the island — a sad reflection of male dominance. She lived in the 5th century and is a Galway Bay saint, being also associated with a place near Kinvara. Her chapel has a feminine quality to it with curved walls and odd stones protruding. Under the cliff face is her well. Close by are the remains of other buildings where you can find some pieces of cross-slabs and a broken quern stone.

Sourney's was a place of pilgrimage in times past. A sacred hawthorn tree was used to hang pieces of cloth as prayer tokens and pilgrims vigilled overnight.

# 5
# Eochaill

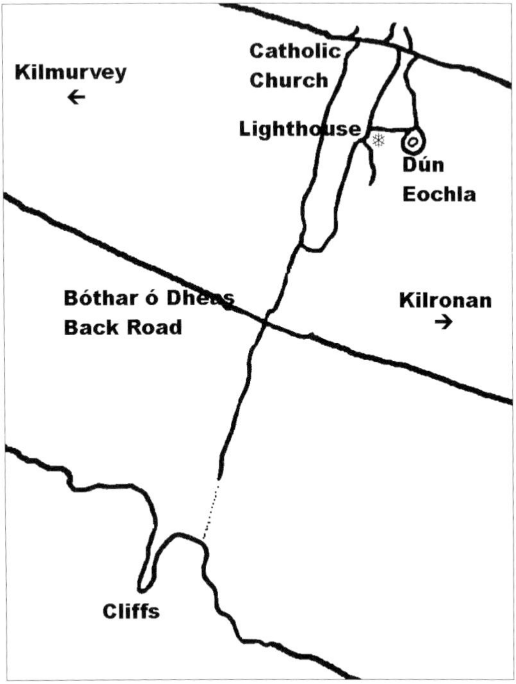


### *Dún Eochla*

Dún Eochla, a ring fort, is approached from the main upper road, half way between Cill Rónáin and Cill Mhuirbhigh. It is at the highest point of the island alongside an old lighthouse and is visible from the road. The turn is signposted and the bóithrín uphill is tarmaced.

It is also possible to access the Dún from a small bóithrín a hundred yards from this turn in the direction of Cill Rónáin. This footpath leads through fields.

Dún Eochla is separate from the lighthouse complex, which is now developed as a folk museum. Walk around the lighthouse wall to get to the Dún.

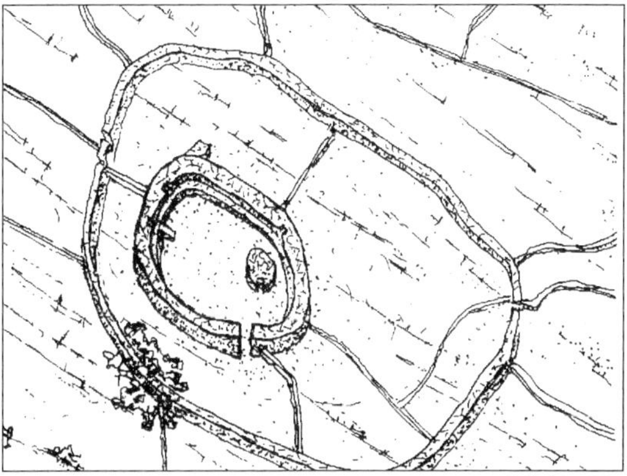

*Dún Eochla*

Dún Eochla gives a commanding view of the eastern part of Inis Mór, including Cill Rónáin and Cill Éinne. From here you can see the other two Aran Islands and the Cliffs of Moher in County Clare. Dún Dubhchathair is also visible from here.

Inside the fort, there are steps in the wall. These rise to the top where there is a walkway along the perimeter. Looking out you will see another thick wall ringing the fort. All of these walls were repaired and rebuilt by the Board of Works in the 1880s and have been maintained ever since. The pile of stones in the middle of the fort may be the result of a tidying up job on two stone huts, similar to those to be seen at Dún Dubhchathair.

The fort was built probably between 550 and 800 AD. However, it may have replaced an older settlement. It was the dwelling place for a small clan or extended family. They built their huts of stone and thatch inside the inner wall and kept their animals within the outer walls.

Inis Mór has the remains of many such forts, not all of them in such good condition. This illustrates just how populated Aran was in earlier times. We today are inclined to think of the Aran Islands as a remote place off the west coast of Europe, but in those days the Aran

## High Places

*In practically every religious tradition, certain mountains and hills have taken on a spiritual significance. In the Judaic tradition, Moses received the Ten commandments on Mount Sinai. In the Christian tradition, Jesus was transfigured on Mount Tabor. In the Celtic tradition, the Lughnasa harvest was celebrated at Croagh Patrick.*

*Lugh is the god of light — the sun. He married Boand, the earth goddess, at Samhain (Halloween). Nine months later they had a child: the harvest at Lughnasa. At Cruachán Aigle (now Croagh Patrick), Lugh lies down with Boand at sunset and rises again at dawn. Those who climbed this mountain overnight symbolically got into bed with them and then celebrated the outcome — the harvest.*

*For the Celts, the Otherworld is not a million miles away but in the here and now. A person can access the Otherworld, disappear into it, fall in love with somebody from it, even have a parent from it. The stories of fairies and leprechauns are part of this tradition but are really a trivialisation of deep insights into spiritual experience.*

*The Celts knew that certain places on the landscape lent themselves to getting in touch with the Otherworld. These were the liminal places. A high place is such a place, especially one where an ancient monument stands. The ancient monuments house the spirits of the Otherworld. The Celtic Gods — the Tuatha Dé Danann — live there.*

Islands were strategically important. Those living on them held the balance of power. This was because the islands spanned the mouth of Galway Bay and all sea faring activity could be monitored and controlled from Aran. In times past, travel by boat was a common means of transport when the inner reaches of the country were often impassable due to forests and bogs.

An esker left behind by the Ice Age divides the country in half and runs from Galway to Dublin. This esker marked the dividing line between different kingdoms. From earliest times, the people who lived north of this esker were the enemies of the people who lived south of it. That enmity continued right through to the 17th century when the 'ferocious' O'Flaherty's of Galway were fighting the O'Brien's of Clare. The battles between Galway and Clare continue on the football and hurling pitches today.

### *A Thin Place*

This ring fort is a liminal or thin place — where the divide between the two worlds is at its thinnest — a place especially favoured by the Celts. Being the high point of the island, it is a place where this world and the other world touch. The fort and its location invite your imagination to take you out of the present time into some other moment of history — when the Celts were celebrating the midsummer festival with a bonfire; when myriads of monks were bustling about their clocháns, small chapels and round tower at Cill Éinne; when the Viking ships were attacking.

Hilltops are for Otherworld meetings, conversations with the Divine, seeing things differently, allowing something new into your life, letting go, clarifying your vision, foreseeing the future, making decisions. Coming down from the mountaintop is a re-entry into the world equipped for a new task.

### *The Lighthouse*

The lighthouse is also known as Britain's Folly. Built in

1818 with enormous labour, it never worked satisfactorily for boats at sea, being too far inland and giving no indication of the length of the island. It was replaced in 1857 by a lighthouse at either end of the island. The buildings around the lighthouse include the signal tower and the residence for the lighthouse keeper. The whole site has now been developed into a folk museum and viewing tower.

### *The Cliffs*

Take the bóithrín that passes the lighthouse and head on out towards the cliffs. As you go, you leave humanity behind and enter an Otherworld. The bóithrín brings you up against stiles in stone walls and eventually leaves you to your fate altogether as you approach the cliff.

You have arrived at a bay dug into the cliff face known as Poll an Iomair. An iomair is a bowl or container and the bay is shaped like one. The cliffs are two hundred feet high at this point. They rise to over three hundred feet (100 metres) at Dún Aonghusa and beyond.

This cliff is where traditionally islanders went fishing for ballaigh (rock fish or wrasse). The line is baited with periwinkle, weighted with lead and lowered over the cliff. A foot is dangled out over the edge to keep the line away from the cliff wall. It takes a sensitive hand to feel the pull of a rockfish in the water below at a height of two hundred feet! These ballaigh were taken home and salted for the winter.

Up to a few generations ago, islanders were accustomed to scaling these cliffs for eggs and birds. A young man was lowered over the edge at dusk, secured to a rope. He climbed into a ledge halfway down the cliff and spent the night gathering eggs and ringing birds' necks. At dawn his co-helpers returned and pulled him up. The dead birds had value for their meat, their feathers and their oil. Razorbills, puffins, guillemots and cormorants all met their fate in this way. Today, the puffins have gone from the site, but the fulmars have taken their place.

### *Eochaill Catholic Church*

Taking a different bóithrín back from the cliffs will lead you down to the main road at Eochaill Catholic Church. This church, opened in 1833, was the first modern church to be built on the island. It replaced a small stone church, the remains of which are to be seen across the road in a field to the north, one field back from the road.

When no other church existed on the island, that is from 1833 to 1905 (when Kilronan church was built), Eochaill church was the parish church and people had to travel up to seven miles to attend Mass on a Sunday. As they walked, often barefoot, they recited prayers they had learned in their childhood. Here is an example: "Toradh agus tairbhe an Aifrinn seo go dtuga tú dúinn agus gach uile Aifreann atá á rá ar fud an domhain mhóir, dúinn féin agus dár gcomhchréatúirí" (The fruit and benefit of this Mass may you give to us, and of every Mass that is being said throughout the big world — to us and our fellow-creatures).

People attended Mass with great piety and continuous repetition of prayers in those days. A woman who attended Mass in Achill island, further north from Aran, had this to say: "The church was packed and never before (or since) have I seen and heard such fervour. The congregation attended Mass in every sense of the word, making the responses aloud with the altar boys, and at the Consecration there was such a cry of welcome to our Lord in the Blessed Sacrament — 'Céad míle fáilte, a Thiarna' (a hundred thousand welcomes, O Lord) — that the tears came to my eyes — and I am not an emotional person."

# 6
# Corrúch

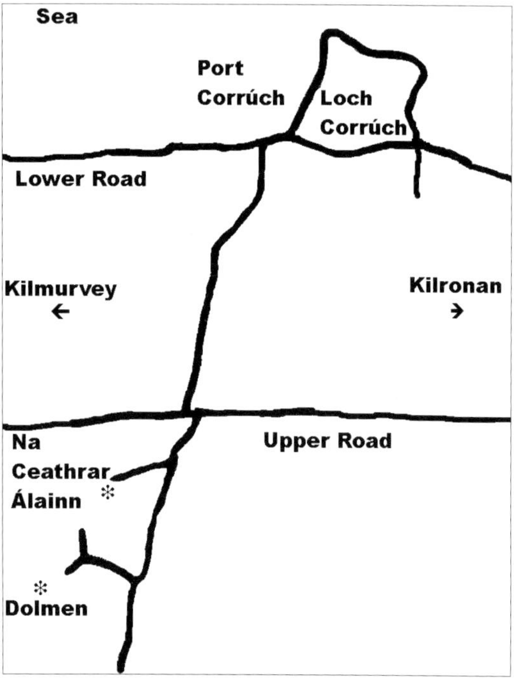


***An Ceathrar Álainn - The Four Comely Saints***

In the village of Corrúch, a signposted bóithrín leads to the monastic settlement known as An Ceathrar Álainn (The Four Comely Saints). Watch out for the white pointer across a stile on the right about a 100 yards up the lane. Crossing a few small fields, following the track and pointers, the old church is visible up ahead of you.

The first unusual feature of this site is the four graves at the gable end of the church, marked by flat slabs and a low wall. Here the remains of St Fursey, St Berchan, St Brendan of Birr and St Conal are buried.

Fursey is one of the greatest of the Irish missionary saints.

*Teampall An Cheathrair Álainn*

When he died in France in the 7th century, his body was held incorrupt in a portico for four years while a magnificent new church in Peronne was being completed to receive him. His connection with Aran is that he was born in Galway. A relic of his body may have been brought here to be buried.

Brendan of Birr was a close friend of Colmcille. It is likely that he studied on Aran before setting up his monastic school in Birr, County Offaly. He is one of the Twelve Apostles of Ireland. Not much is known about Conal or Berchan.

The statue of Mary, the mother of Jesus, in the east gable window was placed there with great ceremony by a local woman, Bríd Gillan, on the occasion of her 100th birthday in 1994. At this time of re-editing, she is still alive, aged 107.

The church itself is medieval and probably replaced an older church. Further up the hill, there are the remains of several clocháns. One of these can be accessed by going back out onto the lane and crossing a stile further up.

### *The Well of the Saints*

Near the four graves, at an opening in a field wall, the main holy well is to be found. This is the well referred to by John Millington Synge in his play 'The Well of the

Saints' and also in his book 'The Aran Islands'. A track goes around the back of this well and comes back out through another hole in the wall to lead one around the church and back to the well. This is the route of the turas deiseal, the traditional prayer round (see page 42).

To do this, take seven stones at the well and do the round seven times as you pray. Each time passing the well, drop a stone alongside it. To finish, kneel down at the well, drink some of the water and bless yourself with it. If you are agile, you could imitate earlier pilgrims and lie on the graves for a few minutes and make your prayer.

### *Standing Stones*

Looking west towards Dún Aonghusa from the gable of the church, you will see two standing stones almost in line. The nearer one is just about accessible from here but the farther one is best accessed from the next bóithrín off the main road. Neither stone has any markings and the farther one is a massive eleven feet high.

### *Traditional Rituals*

The traditional day for visiting An Ceathrar Álainn is August 15th. There is a custom on the island of visiting it three times in succession, on two consecutive Fridays and the Wednesday in between. Up to the early 1900s, this was a popular place of pilgrimage, possibly the most important one on the island. People came from Connemara and further afield to do the rounds, lie overnight on the graves of the four saints, and take back home water from the holy well.

### *The Four Wells*

There are four wells at this site associated with the four saints. The main well is the first and obvious one. The second is to be found on your way out across the track. Having come down off the monastic wall, you cross a field, and then go over a stile turning left onto a track. Just after the track bears right, you will see the well at your feet to the left a foot off the track. This well is noted locally for healing of the eyes.

## Holy Water

*For the Celts, many types of water are holy. Well water is holy because it comes from the entrance to the womb of the earth. Wells therefore are very suitable places for performing baptisms or welcoming or naming ceremonies for children.*

*River water is holy:*
*— because it represents the blood of the goddess Danu or Bríd, whose body is the land of Ireland;*
*— because the river itself represents a goddess. The Shannon is the goddess Sinand. The Boyne is Boand, the white cow goddess;*
*— because every river is a liminal place, a place of transition, where the Otherworld can impinge on human life.*

*Dew water is also holy. The gaelic word drúcht has the same root as draoi, druid, and suggests something magical. The dew is mysterious— no one knows where it comes from or disappears to.*

*Dew is gathered in the month of May, Bealtaine, to beautify women's faces and to promote fertility. A sheet is left out overnight and the dew collected by squeezing it out in the morning. On the eve of Imbolc, February 1st, a cloth called Brat Bhríd, Brigid's Cloak, is placed outside in a similar way. The spirit of Brigid comes on this cloth overnight and it is then used throughout the year for protection and healing.*

*Dew is like the Holy Spirit. In an inspired translation, the gaelic version of the Roman Catholic Eucharistic Prayer II prays for God to bless the gifts 'le drúcht do Spiorad' — 'with the dew of your Spirit'.*

## The Dead

*In the Celtic world, when a person dies, six days must pass while deputations of angels and demons sort out which way the soul must go.*

*Prior to Christianity, the soul was collected by Donn, the god of the dead, who brought it to Teach Donn, an island off the Kerry coast now called Bull Rock.*

*Today, Donn has been replaced by Michael the Archangel. His island, Skellig Michael, is very close to Teach Donn — close enough, no doubt, to divert the souls his way!*

*From here, the soul is led on its journey to various mystical islands where it is purified. The ancient voyage of Bran is such a tale. Brendan the Navigator set out in search of these islands and returned to tell us about some of them in his book 'The Brendan Voyage'.*

*The world of the dead is off to the west, the land of the setting sun. Souls travel along the Golden Road. This road is laid across the sea by the setting sun.*

*Until recent times, grieving over a death on Aran was accompanied by caoineadh, the keening of women. John Millington Synge described keening as 'calling out to the dead with a perpetually recurring chant of sobs'. Women took turns in leading the chant, and bodies swayed to and fro 'possessed for the moment with a profound ecstasy of grief'.*

*Dolmen - Leaba Diarmuid agus Gráinne*

Past this well on the way out, you cross another stile. Turn right here and look at the base of the wall a few yards from the stile. You will see a bullán stone, or holy water font. This is the third 'well'. In reality of course it is not a well, but does hold sacred significance because possibly it was originally used in an earlier church as a holy water font. This would mean it should be used to bring protection and to drive away evil.

In the Christian tradition, water becomes sacred when it is blessed by a priest. However, in earlier times, the sacred water was the water collected as dew early in the morning. This due was collected on cloths and squeezed out into containers. Its mystical quality was due to the fact that its appearance and disappearance on the land could not be explained. An integration of these two traditions could come about by the Christian priest blessing only dew water for the fonts of churches and homes.

The fourth well is the village well, to be found back out on the lane and further up the hill on the left.

***The Dolmen - Leaba Diarmuid agus Gráinne***

Head further up this hill, past the pointer for the clochán. The hill levels out and here you will find a bóithrín to the right. Take this turn and walk over the brow of the hill until you see Dún Aonghusa in the distance. Into the left through the fields you will also see a stone monument.

## The Story of Diarmuid and Gráinne

*Diarmuid was a soldier in the Fianna — the mighty army of Fionn MacCumhail. Gráinne was a princess — the daughter of the High King at Tara, Cormac Mac Airt.*

*Fionn MacCumhail had asked for Gráinne's hand in marriage and, to everyone's surprise, Gráinne had accepted. However, she had never really laid eyes on Fionn and was only going on his reputation. When she saw him at the betrothal ceremony she realised her mistake. He was twice her age and his body was scarred and deformed from battle.*

*Gráinne devised a plan. Passing a sleeping potion in some wine to the main table, where Fionn and her father sat, she put all the powerful people in the room to sleep and then went looking for Diarmuid, a man she had always had her eye on.*

*She put a geis on Diarmuid to elope with her. A geis is like a spell. Once it is on you, it is extremely dangerous not to abide by it. You will be utterly destroyed. Diarmuid's friends advised him to go with Gráinne and promised to help.*

*Fionn woke up and found them gone. His pride had been damaged. Nothing would stop him from recovering his lost bride. Every night Diarmuid and Gráinne were forced to sleep in a different bed. They travelled through all parts of Ireland.*

...to page 61

...from page 60

*Meanwhile, Diarmuid had tried to remain faithful to Fionn his commander, despite the geis. He would not make love to Gráinne because she was promised to Fionn. One day they crossed a stream. The water splashed up onto the inside of Gráinne's thigh. She taunted Diarmuid: "the trickle of water is more adventurous than you are when it comes to love". That night Diarmuid yielded to his love for her and they became husband and wife.*

*After sixteen years of chase, no side had been victorious. Fionn, getting older, had been convinced by Aonghus, the god of love, to call a truce. Diarmuid and Gráinne settled down as husband and wife in Rath Gráinne, Keshcorran, County Sligo. They reared four sons and one daughter.*

*After many years of peace, Fionn, apparently reconciled, came to visit. He and Diarmuid went hunting together and Diarmuid got killed by the wild boar of Ben Bulben. Fionn was implicated in his death because he did not come to his aid in time.*

*In the final chapter of the story, Fionn again wooed Gráinne and slowly won her over. Meanwhile, her children planned to do battle with Fionn to avenge their father's death. Fionn and Gráinne eventually married and this prevented the final massacre of Fionn and his troops. A peace settlement was hammered out and this ended the pursuit of Diarmuid and Gráinne.*

This is a dolmen (burial site) and is about four thousand years old.

A stile leads across the wall from the lane, and then you have to do a bit of clambering to get over the next wall which brings you down to the dolmen.

This dolmen is wedge shaped and faces the setting sun. It may have been the burial place for one very important person, or for numerous people whose bodies were first corrupted or burned and whose bones were buried here. When in use, it was covered in soil and looked like a mound.

This is the leaba (bed) of Diarmuid and Gráinne. They slept here one night during their elopement, as they evaded the chase led by Fionn MacCumhail. A similar Leaba lies on Inis Meáin.

Dolmens, and other such mounds throughout Ireland, are places where the gods and Otherworld spirits of the Tuatha Dé Danann live. When the Tuatha Dé Danann were defeated by the Celts, they agreed to live underground. Manannán, the god of the sea, was given the task of issuing them with a place to live beneath the mounds and sacred hills of Ireland. It is certain that some members of the sídhe (Otherworld fairies) live here at this dolmen.

### *Loch Chorrúch*

From Corrúch village, Loch Chorrúch is approached via a bóithrín almost directly opposite the bóithrín leading uphill to An Ceathrar Álainn. It can also be approached via the Lower Road coming from either Cill Rónáin or Cill Mhuirbhigh.

This is a fresh water lake, slightly salted by seepage from the sea. Where the lake meets the road, a spring well offers fresh water for cattle and also feeds the lake. Depending on the season, many different types of birds can be seen here. Regular residents include mute swans, shellducks, mallards, herons and waterhens. Whooper swans often appear in the winter. There are eels in the lake but not much else. Local people claim to have seen an otter now and again.

A turn off the road on the Cill Rónáin side of the lake will take you around the far side and out onto the dúirling (stone beach). On your travels you may be blessed with the sighting of a lizard sunning itself on the warm limestone rock, or of a stoat bounding like a German sausage on legs in front of you.

### *Port Chorrúch*

A dúirling (stone beach) separates Loch Chorrúch from Port Chorrúch. Together they give a contrasting view of nature from fresh water to salt water. Port Chorrúch hosts seabirds such as cormorants, black-backed gulls, kittiwakes, herring gulls, terns, oyster catchers, ringed plovers, choughs, redshanks and dunlins. The choughs are pigeon sized birds, jet black with curved red beaks and red legs. They are relatively rare, even on Inis Mór.

The bay itself hosts a large colony of seals, sometimes up to forty of them. When the tide is low they bask on the exposed rocks or cavort in the shallow water. At other times, a careful scan of the bay will usually locate a few heads above the water.

The ruined building close to the bay is the remains of An Teach Mór, the seaweed factory built in 1865 for drying and burning seaweed to kelp. The kelp was sold into Galway for the extraction of iodine.

# 7
# Fearann-a-Choirce
# and
# Gort na gCapall

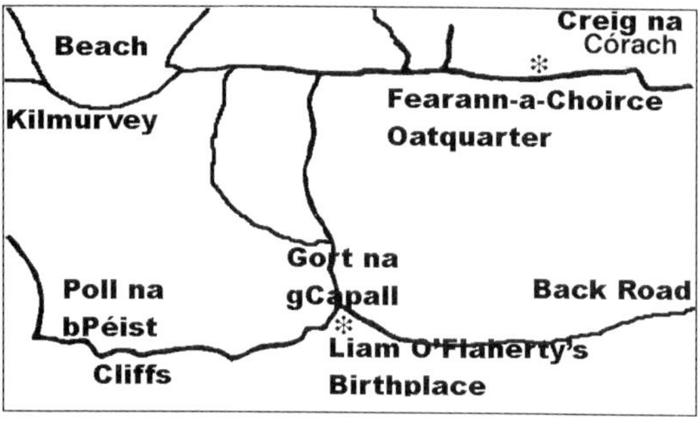


*Fearann-a-Choirce / Oatquarter*

Fearann-a-Choirce is the village on the steep hill leading down to Cill Mhuirbhigh beach. After you pass the school and Coláiste Ó Direáin (an Irish language summer college), the road takes a steep descent. Before you reach the pub further down the hill, notice a plaque on the wall on the right hand side. The inscription reads 'Creig na Córach' (the crag of justice). Herein lies a tale:

Enda, as we have seen, had difficulty establishing his jurisdiction over all of the monks on the island. Some of the monks wanted an anarchic system, where each of them followed their own lights. The dispute could not be resolved and so all of the participants, including Enda, fasted against God. The dispute ended in favour of Enda (see page 18) .

However, Enda continued to have problems, especially with the monks who lived furthest away from him at the other end of the island. A large monastic settlement had developed at what is now known as Na Seacht dTeampaill (The Seven Churches). St Breacán was the abbot there and he insisted that Enda divide the island into two jurisdictions. Enda reluctantly complied and it remained only to find the dividing boundary.

It was arranged that Enda and Breacán would arise on a particular day at dawn, celebrate Mass and walk towards one another until they met. Their meeting point would mark the dividing boundary.

Enda slept on top of the hill at Teampall Bheanáin where he would see the sun rising earlier and so get a good start. Breacán did worse — he took a horse to make up the ground more quickly. However, Enda having druidic eyes, spotted that Breacán was cheating and put a spell on the horse, rivetting its feet to the rock at this spot.

The marks of the hooves are there to this day, buried beneath the tarmac. But until the 1880s, when the road works were carried out, all those passing could see the hoof marks and remember the story — reminding themselves that cheating does not pay. In the 1940s, Fr Killeen erected the plaque. Creig na Córach means the crag of justice.

### *Gort na gCapall*

Travelling on down the hill past the pub on the right, a turn to the left will lead you to Gort na gCapall (the field of the horses). This is the only village on the south side of the island. It has a remoteness that none of the others have. Here the writer Liam O'Flaherty was born and reared. His short stories capture beautifully the world of his childhood and youth. To find the house where he was born, go into the village until you get to the junction. The main road goes left but if you go straight ahead, the house is immediately on your left.

### *Poll na bPéist*

Follow this lane past Liam O'Flaherty's birthplace out of the village and down towards the cliffs and shore. The track comes out at a narrow, rock strewn beach and a slip built in 1956. The slip is in a very dangerous place and is no longer used.

Turn right and follow the coastline. As the cliff rises it emerges into three levels. It is not advised to ever take the lowest level. It may be necessary to stay at the top level, if the tide is in. Taking the middle level requires careful assessment of the situation, particularly if the sea is rough. People have been taken unawares here and some have had lucky escapes, not without injury.

Whether you take the high level or the middle level, it still leads to Poll na bPéist (Worm Hole), although on the high level you will have to peer over the edge to see it.

Poll na bPéist is a blow-hole created by the sea putting enormous pressure on the roof of a cave initially formed beneath it. However, the shape of the hole and its theatrical setting in a curve of sheer cliff invites the imagination to come up with a better name than Worm Hole. The Sea-Monster's Lair would be more appropriate.

In almost every cultural tradition there are stories of monsters in lakes or holes such as this. They fascinate and enthral us, adults and children, because somewhere inside us all is a monster who could get out of control and do unimaginable damage to ourselves and the world around us. In these stories, the monster is usually killed, driven out or tamed.

At Poll na bPéist the water level surges up and down angrily even in the most settled weather. This is the place to come face to face with the monster within us.

A note of warning — it is not safe to swim here.

# 8
# Cill Mhuirbhigh - Kilmurvey

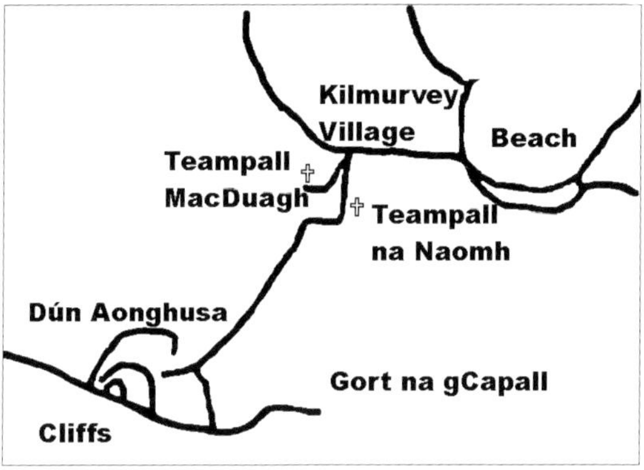


You can travel from Cill Rónáin to Cill Mhuirbhigh via the Lower Road (turn right at Joe Watty's Pub) or the Upper Road. Either way you arrive at Cill Mhuirbhigh Beach — one of the finest beaches on Inis Mór — which has Blue Flag status.

Cill Mhuirbhigh means 'church among the sand-dunes'. However the church has long since disappeared. The beach was one of the main locations for the film 'The Man of Aran', filmed by Robert Flaherty in 1932 and 1933. The twin thatched cottage built for the film can be seen on the west side of the beach. It is now a restaurant and Bed and Breakfast. On the pier itself is a small building originally built and used for developing the film. The film is on show daily at Ionad Árann, the heritage centre in Kilronon. Video copies can also be bought there.

Taking a left at the fork in the road at the west side of the beach, you arrive at Cill Mhuirbhigh village. The first house you come to, on the right, was initially a Protestant Bible school, and later a constabulary barracks. It is now a private dwelling. Behind the thatched craft shops is the large Conneely home, now derelict. This began as a cottage but grew into a guest house, post office and shop. Many of Ireland's intelligentsia spent summers here in the 1920's and 30's, as part of the language revival movement that was going on at that time. It is said that Brendan Behan met his future wife Beatrice on Cill Mhuirbhigh Beach while both were staying here.

Next to Conneely's is Kilmurvey House, a big stone Georgian building, now a guest house. This house was built by Patrick O'Flaherty in the 1850s. Patrick was a Catholic middle-man who had leased large tracts of Aran land from the owners of the island, the Digbys of County Kildare. He then sub-let the land to tenants. Both he and a land-agent for Digbys called Thompson, who lived at Killeany Lodge, were the main rent-collectors on the island. Patrick O'Flaherty and his son after him were also appointed Justices of the Peace on the island. This gave them the power to hold court, prosecute and jail islanders.

In 1922 the Irish Government's Land Commission bought the island from the Digby's for £13,721. The land was then divided up among island families, all of whom now own their own farms of 20-40 acres. In front of Kilmurvey House, which was left with about 300 acres, the fields are large and lush, whereas beyond them are the more common postage stamp size plots. Thus the history is written into the landscape. Kilmurvey House is now owned by an island family.

### *Teampall Mhic Duach*

Beside Kilmurvey House, in its grounds, is an old church called Teampall Mhic Duach. It is called after St Colman Mac Duach of County Clare. Many island men are called Colman after him. The three west of Ireland saints - St Mac Duach, St Mac Cartan and St Mac Dara all had the same mother and are so named after their respective fathers.

Colman Mac Duach had a brother Guaire who was the king of Connacht. One day, after a long Lenten fast, a cleric in Colman's monastery in County Clare longed for meat and had none. Colman prayed that an angel would

*Teampall Mhic Duach*

bring it to him. The angels visited Colman's brother Guaire who was at the time sitting down to his Easter feast. They took the dishes from the table and led the king and his men on a chase down the six mile stretch of road to Colman's monastery where the meat was delivered to the hungry cleric. The road is known since as the Road of the Dishes. It stretches from near Kinvara to the present remains of Colman's main monastery at Kilmacduach. Local folklore says the cleric died of over-eating.

The church is probably 11th century, the chancel a later addition. Near the west gable is a cross-inscribed standing stone. An unusual carving of a horse can be seen on the west cornerstone of the north wall at about eye height.

Colman lived in the 7th century and so pre-dates the present building. Like many other founders, he spent some time in his youth on Aran with Enda. This church and another church close by formed part of a monastic enclosure that incorporated numerous other buildings. A holy well, now dried up, lies in the grounds of Kilmurvey House to the south and the remains of a caiseal (cashel wall) are also to be seen to the south.

### *Teampall na Naomh*

Out the main gate of Kilmurvey House and across the

*Dún Aonghusa*

road behind the converted stables, now a cafeteria, lies Teampall na Naomh (the church of the saints). A small chapel, its presence makes more sense in the context of a larger monastic enclosure which included both it, Teampall Mhic Duach and other buildings.

### *Dún Aonghusa*

It does not matter whether you are rich or poor, everybody has to walk the last half mile up the winding hill to Dún Aonghusa. Visiting Dún Aonghusa is a pilgrimage to a sacred site, where you are almost guaranteed a spiritual experience. Going on foot is part of the required ritual.

As you climb, you can marvel at the many beautiful wild flowers next to the path — the bloody cranesbills, the orchids, the wild roses — depending on the time of year. As you near the top and pass through the first and second cashel wall, the view begins to unfold behind and to the left. But nothing can compare with the experience from the innermost cashel.

Entering the inner sanctum of Dún Aonghusa is like entering the Holy of Holies of the Jewish Temple in Jerusalem at the time of Christ. In Jesus' day only priests such as Zechariah (Jn.1:5-25) were allowed enter. Today at Dún Aonghusa all of us share in this priesthood.

At the centre of the inner cashel is a stone platform, a stage that turns the tiered cashel walls into rows of seat-

## The Story of Aonghus

*Aonghus is the Celtic god of love. He is known as Aonghus Óg, young Aonghus, because he is eternally youthful. He is a great hurley player and lives at Newgrange, Co. Meath. Dún Aonghusa is his summer residence. From Dún Aonghusa one can reach Tír na nÓg, the land of eternal youth.*

*Aonghus' parents were Dagda — the leader of the Tuatha de Danann, and Boand — the river goddess of the Boyne. Dagda had straddled the river to make love to Boand, and, to fool her husband, had suspended the coming on of night and squeezed nine months into a day, so that Aonghus was both conceived and born on the one day.*

*Aonghus fell in love with Caer whom he saw in a dream. It took him a year to find her. She lived alternately as a beautiful woman and as a swan, a year at a time. Aonghus went to Loch Béal Dragan in County Tipperary and saw her there among a hundred and fifty swans. He turned into a swan himself and joined her and they both flew to Newgrange to live. There they became the protectors of loving couples. When Diarmuid and Gráinne were in trouble, Aonghus came to their aid* *(see page 60-61)**.*

*Aonghus has four bright birds flying about his head. These are his four kisses. When these birds sing, all the youths and maidens of Ireland are charmed and love springs up in their hearts.*

ing for those attending. It is a spectacular setting, with a 100 metre sheer drop off the edge, for any type of ceremony, celebration or ritual.

The contemporary ritual at this site is to crawl out on your belly to the edge of the cliff and look down. It is a fitting posture for the expression of awe, wonder and a certain fear that most people feel.

Archaeological evidence has shown that this area was inhabited, on and off, as far back as 1500 BC. There may have been a hill fort here before the present walls were erected. But whatever buildings were or were not here in the past, it is the site itself which gives the shot of electricity that runs up the spine. While the Greeks built Temples and the Romans built roads and aqueducts, the Celts concentrated on marking the sacred spots of the landscape. Dún Aonghusa marks one of their finest discoveries.

### *Chevaux de Frise*

Coming out of the inner cashel of Dún Aonghusa, turn left and follow the wall around until to your right you see an opening in the second cashel wall. This leads to an opening in a third wall, through which you will see the defence system of the fort, the Chevaux de Frise referred to earlier in relation to Dún Dubhchathair. Literally this means the Frisians' horses. The Frisians of northern Europe did not have horses, so they placed large stones in the ground at various awkward angles to prevent the horses of the enemy getting through.

One wonders where the cavalry charge might have come from on such a small isolated island! The defence system is quite extensive, but like everything else about the fort, it may have been built more to express the status of those who ruled from it than for practical purposes.

The people who lived at Dún Aonghusa were people of wealth and status. They had to be to have had the workforce available to them to build the walls and chev-

## The Five Invasions of Ireland.

*To avoid the Flood, a woman called Cessair arrived in Ireland, having been tipped off by her grandfather Noah. She reckoned that a land without humans, and therefore without sin and evil, would not come under God's angry hand. She and her companions eventually died and the land was left fallow again.*

*After the Flood, Partholon the Greek arrived with his companions. He introduced the first cattle to Ireland. All of his descendants died of the plague between two Mondays in May, except a man called Tuán who could shape-change.*

*Next came Nemed, a druidic character and forerunner of the Tuatha Dé Danann. His name means a sacred place. He came up against the nasty Formorians who used Ireland as a base and eventually he got driven out.*

*The next invasion was by a race of people called the Fir Bolg (bag men). When they were slaves in Greece they were forced to carry bags of soil to the poorer regions to improve the agriculture. They divided Ireland into five provinces.*

*After 37 years the Fir Bolg were defeated by the Tuatha Dé Danann. They retreated to various islands including Rathlin and Aran. Aonghus, their leader, built Dún Aonghusa. When St Enda came to Aran he had to deal with one of their leaders — Corban. The Tuatha Dé Danann brought with them gods and goddesses and gave Ireland its mythology.*

*So, there were five invasions of Ireland before the Celts. After the Celts arrived, the Tuatha Dé Danann chose to live under the ground of Ireland where they inhabit the sacred places.*

aux de frise. The archaeological survey conducted in the 1990's unearthed bronze jewellery, pottery, and other artefacts confirming this opinion. A small number of families lived within the inner cashel wall in houses made of stone walls and thatched roofs. However, it is probable that a larger number of families lived outside the Dún but gathered there in times of festivities and in times of attack. One can think of the Dún therefore as operating on three levels: domestic, religious, and defence.

The Celts had various rituals for the celebration of festivals. Chief among the festivals were the four to mark the changes of season: Imbolc, Bealtaine, Lúnasa, and Samhain. But the king or chieftain also held an annual festival to gather all his clan together, and many competitions and tournaments took place at this festival. There would also have been ritual celebrations for the crowning of a new king and for weddings. All of these ceremonies could well have been conducted at Dún Aonghusa.

The large platform of stone in the centre of the inner walled area is clearly not man-made. However, it may have been quarried at the edges. Archaeologists think this may have happened as late as the 5th century A.D. Close to the stone platform is an oblong stone structure sunk into the ground. This is the remains of a fulacht fia (a cooking site). The fulacht fia was filled with water. A fire nearby heated some large rounded stones which, when red hot, were rolled into the water to boil it. Food was then cooked in the boiling water.

It is said that Aonghus, the leader of the Fir Bolg, ruled from here, after being vanquished by the Tuatha Dé Danann. This may also explain how the fort got its name. However, the original Aonghus is Aonghus Óg, the ever-young God of Love from Celtic mythology. He is a more fitting patron and protector of the mystical Dún.

The Visitor Centre for Dun Aonghusa provides a lot more detailed information, and Dúchas guides are at the site to answer questions.

# 9
# Sruthán

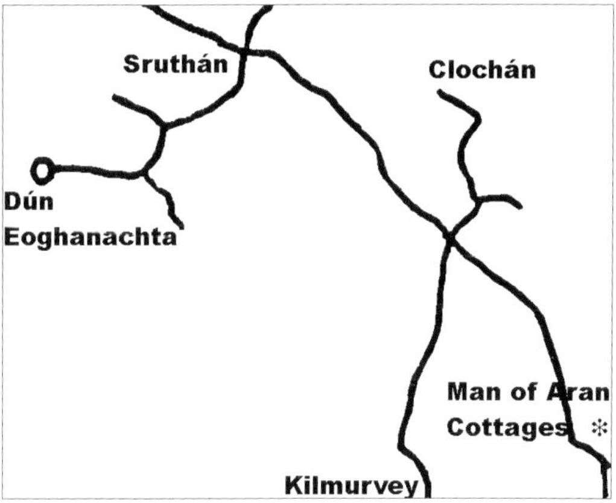


### *'Man of Aran' Cottages*

The 'Man of Aran' Cottages are at the northwest of Cill Mhuirbhigh Beach. Follow the road around the beach to the northwest tip. The road then turns away from the bay and immediately on your right are the thatched cottages. In fact, it is one double cottage, built that way to accommodate the cameras in one while the action took place in the other.

Robert Flaherty filmed the 'Man of Aran' over a two year period in 1932-33. For the film, he used native islanders Maggie Dirrane, Tiger King and Mikleen Dillane in starring roles, which led to their being feted in London and New York. His film captured the starkness of Aran life, a constant struggle against the elements. Central to the film is a whale-hunt, a practice which had in fact died out almost a hundred years before the film was made. The film may be viewed and purchased at the Heritage Centre in Cill Rónáin.

### *Clochán na Carraige — Beehive Hut*

Travelling west from the 'Man of Aran' Cottages, turn

right off the road at a signposted crossroads. The bóithrín leads, via some white pointers, to a beehive hut — Clochán na Carraige.

This is the finest example of a clochán on Inis Mór. Many others are to be found on the island, but in a much more delapidated state. This hut is intact with a corbelled roof and two doorways. It is oval outside, but oblong inside.

The building is difficult to date as it is built of drystone, nonetheless you can presume it is early Christian. You can easily imagine a hermit living here. In the Celtic tradition, hermits or anchorites lived alone but belonged to a monastic community. The monastic community in this case was probably Na Seacht dTeampaill.

The hut was covered in soil and grass, giving it added insulation. Animals were kept at one end. If a fire was lit, one of the flat stones on the roof was removed to let the smoke out. Doors were mats made of straw that could be jammed into the opening to keep out the draught.

### *Dún Eoghanachta*

Dún Eoghanachta is visible on a hill on the left as one heads west from Clochán na Carraige. A signposted turn off the road leads eventually onto a track through fields to the fort. The fort is in good condition with walls intact and the remains of three rectangular clocháns in the enclosure.

The Eoghanacht (pronounced Onacht) were a people who held the kingship of Cashel and ruled most of Munster at the time Christianity came to Ireland. By the 5th century they had conquered County Clare. It is probably at this time or earlier that the fort Dún Eoghanachta was built and gets its name from them. The Eoghanacht were replaced in the 10th century by Brian Boru's people, the Dál gCais. Brian Boru, a Kennedy, became first king of Munster and then High King of Ireland in 1002, defeating the Vikings at the Battle of Clontarf in 1014.

## The Hermit Tradition

*The Irish hermit tradition goes back to the example and inspiration of Paul of Thebes and Anthony of Egypt in the 3rd century. These men chose the desert in which to live as a reaction to city life and gradually inspired others to follow suit. When their biographies were written in the 4th century, the Irish monks eagerly read them and sought for similar desert places in Ireland. There are places in Ireland called díseart (desert) to this day.*

*However, the Irish hermits were not seeking to escape the depravity of city life. There were no cities, nor even towns, in Ireland at the time. Irish monks sought to be heroes, just as their Celtic warrior forebears had done. In the Christian tradition, heroism meant death by martyrdom, not death on the battle field. Death by martyrdom, red martyrdom as it was called, was hard to come by in Ireland, as there was no persecution of the faith. So the monks invented other forms:*
*— white martyrdom as the martyrdom of exile*
*— green martyrdom as a heroic form of penitence and self-denial.*

*The hermit was trying to prove his love for Christ by being a green martyr, that is by living a life of extreme penance. A hermit or anchorite was generally a member of a monastic community but lived at some distance from it. As monastic communities in Ireland developed, the role of*

...to page 78

*Beehive Hut - Clochán na Carraige*

...from page 77
*anchorite became an essential element of every monastery and was often kept within certain families. Sometimes the role passed from father to son.*

*This may seem surprising, but celibacy was not promoted seriously within Christianity until the 12th century. Hermits were not necessarily celibate, even during the Céilí Dé reform movement in Ireland of the 8th to 10th centuries.*

*Some records in the Annals of the Four Masters, a secular chronicle of events, illustrate this point. According to these records, Eoghan was an anchorite (hermit) at Clonmacnoise who died in 845. His great grandson became bishop of Clonmacnoise and died 953. The bishop's son, Eoghan's great-great grandson, took the role again of anchorite at Clonmacnoise and died in 1005. Eoghan's father was abbot of Louth and his grandfather abbot of Armagh.*

*An anchorite was obliged by the rules of hospitality to offer overnight bed and food to those passing by. He or she was also available to give counsel. Some had guesthouses nearby to house those seeking help.*

*Dún Eoghanachta*

Below the fort to the north-east are the remains of a monastic settlement — clocháns, cashel wall and chapel. However, only the outline of these can be seen. The place is called Cill Comhla but nothing is known of Comhla or Comhal. It may be that his bones are buried in the triangular reliquary standing to the south-west of the ruins. Two rectangular slabs lean against one another (broken) and triangular stones fill in each end (one missing).

This slab-shrine was a particularly Irish creation for holding the bones of holy people. As a place of veneration and pilgrimage it parallels the leaba or rectangular slab lying flat on the ground that marked the grave of a saint. Visiting the graves of saints and doing the rounds was an important aspect of medieval pilgrimage.

## The Fourteen Villages of Inis Mór

*There are fourteen villages or townlands on Inis Mór, each with its own name. Each was founded close to a well. When people lived without piped water and needed to fetch water every day, constructing a house close to that well was a wise move. In many of these villages there is also a holy well or sacred site close by. This facilitated people to make just the one trip from the house every day, combining the fetching of domestic water with making their daily turas - or prayer rounds.*

*Every village also has a bonfire site. This is the place where the St John's Eve celebrations are held every year. A bonfire is lit at dusk on June 23rd and is kept lighting until dawn the following morning. All the people of the village, young and old, gather around the bonfire and share food and drink, music and dancing. It is of course a midsummer night festival, long predating Christianity or John the Baptist. But the Christian layer of meaning indicates the Celtic influence on the Christian calendar.*

*The birth of John the Baptist is celebrated at the summer solstice. The birth of Christ is celebrated at the winter solstice. John the Baptist was six months older that Jesus (Lk.1:36). John the Baptist said about Jesus: "He must increase; I must decrease". After the summer solstice, the sun begins to decrease; after the winter solstice, the sun begins to increase.*

# 10
# Eoghanacht to Bun Gabhla

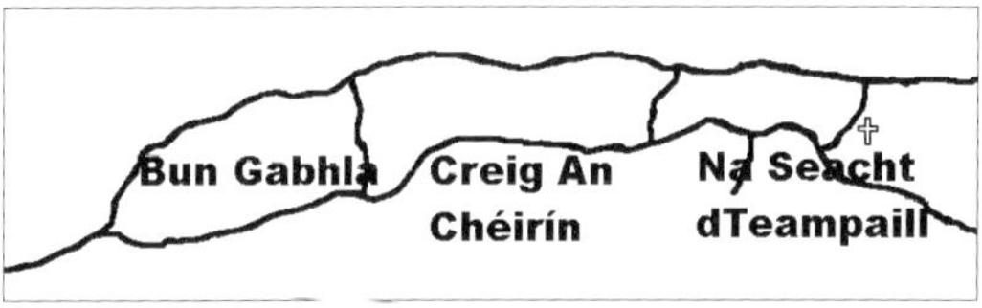


### *Na Seacht dTeampaill - The Seven Churches*

Na Seacht dTeampaill (the Seven Churches) is the finest example of a monastic settlement on Inis Mór. Most of the buildings remain standing, there are some interesting early grave-stones and cross-inscribed slabs, and the broken pieces of three impressive Celtic crosses can be seen — giving a clear indication of the monastery's high status as a place of pilgrimage.

There are in fact only two churches here — the rest of the buildings being domestic in nature. Nonetheless, it was quite common to have numerous churches associated with a monastery. At Cill Éinne, six churches were recorded there at one time. This may be because the ideal size of a monastic community was thirteen, an abbot and twelve monks, following Christ and his twelve apostles. When Celtic monastic settlements grew big, they probably still kept to units of thirteen, each with its own church.

The main church is Teampall Bhreacáin (church of St Breacán). This is the largest building on the site. In the south-western corner is the other church, Teampall an Phoill, literally the church in the hollow or pool.

### *St Breacán*

Breacán came to Aran in the late 5th or early 6th century — around the same time as Enda. He was a son of the king of the Dál gCais in County Clare. This made him of

*Artist's Impression of The Seven Churches*

*Artist: Anne Korff*

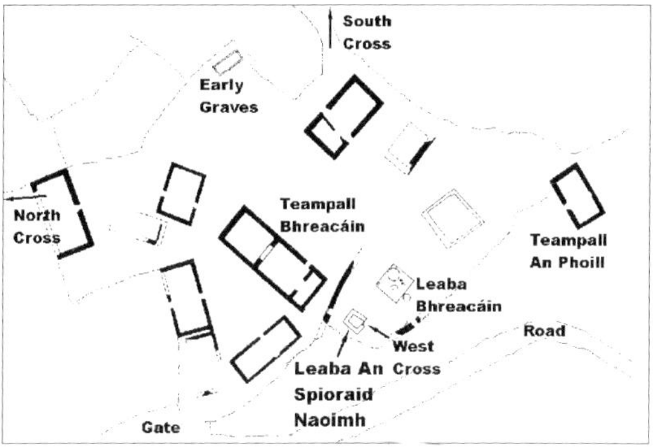


*General plan of The Seven Churches*

equal status to Enda, the king of Oriel's son. It is said that when he came to this place, he had to destroy a pagan idol, Breacáin, and then took his name. He turned the pagan site into a Christian díseart. The original name for Na Seacht dTeampaill is Díseart Bhreacáin, Breacán's desert retreat.

Like many an Aran saint, Breacán is associated also with places on the mainland around Galway Bay — Kilbreckan in Co. Clare and Cill Bhriocáin in Ros Muc, Connemara. He is also believed to be connected with Ardbraccan in County Meath and because of this is known as Breacán of the Two Places.

The story of Breacán dividing the island with St Enda (pages 64-65) portrays him as a tough character. This image is confirmed in a 15th century poem which quotes him saying: "My blessing and my lasting blessing on the family of brave Mael Domhnaigh, may their enemies not destroy them – provided they pay my taxes." And: "A dispute arose between me and Ciarán ... I left Dooras without water. Boldly I cursed the cows of Dooras when they would feel the torment of thirst at the onset of bulling and lactation." Many Irish saints were like this — as quick to curse as to bless. They were seen as people who had power. This power was a recognised inner authority that demanded respect and put them into leadership positions.

*Teampall Bhreacáin*

Breacán's grave, close to Teampall Bhreacáin (see map), has been a place of pilgrimage and homage. A broken grave slab lying at the edge of a rectangular enclosure has his name inscribed on it.

Next to the grave is Leaba an Spioraid Naoimh (the Bed of the Holy Spirit) with the remains of the broken West Cross at its head. Continuous streams of pilgrims who came here prayed at this leaba, at Breacán's grave, and at other graves, crosses and wells throughout the site. They prayed at each station by doing the rounds and saying penitential prayers. The crosses were painted in many colours, making the designs and images on them a lot clearer.

This area of the site was set aside for the pilgrims and was separated from the rest of the monastery by an enclosing wall. The entrance door to the monastery and most of the enclosing wall is still standing. Where the wall has collapsed, the foundations of it are still to be seen.

Pilgrimage to Aran probably reached its zenith around the 12th century, but continued on for hundreds of years after that. Around 1543, a certain Heneas Mac Nichaill strangled his son and was obliged to visit over half a dozen holy places including Aran in atonement for his

## Penitential Pilgrimage

*The tradition of penitential pilgrimage has continued in Ireland up to the present day. On the last Sunday of July each year, up to 50,000 people climb Croagh Patrick, Ireland's sacred mountain, near Westport, County Mayo. Some of these pilgrims go in their bare feet. Until recently, the climb was done during the night.*

*Lough Derg is a small island in County Donegal to which thousands of people travel every year to do a 3-day penitential pilgrimage. They arrive, fasting from all food since midnight the night before, and remove their shoes and socks. Their first night on the island in vigil i.e. without sleep. However, on the second night they are given a bed and allowed eight hours sleep.*

*Throughout the island, which is very small, various stations mark the places where pilgrims stop to do the rounds. They queue to await their turn, and then perform the turas deiseal around the station (see page 42), saying the traditional prayers, and often accompanying them with bodily gestures. Various ceremonies are also held in the church. Once during each day they may go to the dining room, but only to receive a cup of black tea and some dry biscuits.*

*On their final morning, there are more stations and then it is time to put on their shoes and socks and take the boat trip off the island. However, the fast must continue until midnight of that third day.*

## Celtic Monasteries

*At one point in history, there was a real possibility that the Celtic Church would take over from Rome as the dominant ecclesiastical power in Europe. St Columbanus, who died in Bobbio, Italy, in 615, was the spearhead. During his lifetime he and his disciples founded over 100 Celtic monasteries throughout Europe. Many other Celtic monks, men and women, followed the same path. Their names and the remains of their foundations are scattered throughout Europe.*

*This was not an evangelical movement, much less a colonial movement. The monks were not trying to take over or build an empire. Their motivation was white martyrdom, a willingness to leave home in order to perfect their Christian life in exile.*

*They were responding to the gospel imperative: "You are the salt of the earth. But if salt becomes tasteless, what can make it salty again? ... You are the light of the world ... your light must shine in the sight of men ..." (Mt.5:13-16). The goal was Christian perfection, and the fruit was evangelisation.*

*In general, the Irish monks were welcome in Europe. In order to settle in a region, they had to obtain the permission of the local rulers, if not their invitation. However, they did step on the toes of the European bishops, who resented their inroads and their successes. It was not the custom of the Irish monks to consult the bishops, as this had never been done in Ireland.*

*At an early stage in Columbanus' itinerary tension with the bishops resulted in his deportation back to Ireland.*

...to page 87

...from page 86

*Only a storm prevented his arrival home. Instead he was shipwrecked further down the French coast and continued his pilgrim journey.*

*Eventually, the Celtic monks became a real threat to the ecclesiastical power structures, centred mainly in Rome. This led to steps being taken by Rome to have them brought into line.*

*Rome's strategy was to take the Benedictine model of monasticism, little known outside Italy at the time, and make it the standard model of all religious life. Gradually the Celtic model gave way to the Benedictine model. Rules, liturgy, language, dress and tonsure, became universalised.*

*What had distinguished Celtic monasticism was that the emphasis was not on renunciation of the world but on enrichment of the world. The Irish monasteries were situated at crossroads and accessible places. Even Aran was accessible and not at all remote in the minds of earlier peoples. Irish monasteries grew into towns and villages, and even cities.*

*But perhaps the real threat to Rome was that Celtic monasteries were largely independent of one another and of any church control. There was no authority structure higher than the local abbot or abbess. Monasteries were subject only to their founders and their coarbs — the abbots and abbesses who succeeded them.*

*And so, with the eclipse of the Celtic model, ecclesiastical diversity gave way to a worldwide monoculture.*

Teampall an Phoill

sin. In 1607 the Pope granted a plenary indulgence to all who visited the churches of Aran on certain feastdays.

Aran was probably part of a pilgrimage route that included other places such as Skellig Michael in Kerry, Croagh Patrick in Mayo, Inishmurray in Sligo, and Glencolmcille in Donegal — all accessible by sea. For a growing number of people, these pilgrim routes are re-opening, although people now travel by land and air.

### *Teampall Bhreacáin*

In the west gable of Teampall Bhreacáin it is possible to see the outline of an earlier gable that was much smaller. Different parts of the church were constructed during different centuries. The church however, like all Celtic churches, is built on an east-west axis. The narrow window above the altar on the east gable is designed to receive the light from the rising sun of Easter morning, thereby commemorating the resurrection of Christ. As always, there is a window also on the south wall close to the altar. This is designed to receive light from the sun as it travels south of the church throughout the day, and to cast that light on the altar. One has to imagine the church with a thatched roof and therefore in darkness, except for the light cast by these two windows.

### *Inscribed Stone Pillars*

In the east corner of Na Seacht dTeampaill are four inscribed stone pillars marking a number of graves behind them. These pillars are the oldest on the site. The stone on the left has a cross carved on it. The base of the cross is a three-pronged fork. This would suggest that it is an imitation of a metal cross. Metal crosses were carried in procession and the prongs allowed them to be stuck into the ground when the procession stopped.

One cross-inscribed pillar has the inscription TOMAS AP. This stone was originally inside Teampall Bhreacáin and was moved to this position in recent years. It may refer to Thomas the abbot (ab is Gaelic for abbot, and ap may be an older spelling or a misspelling), or Thomas the Apostle. If the latter, then it is a memorial stone and not a grave stone, unless a relic of St Thomas was brought to Aran.

***VII ROMANI***

Another cross-inscribed pillar has the inscription VII ROMANI. There are numerous possible explanations for this inscription.

It may refer to seven pilgrims from Rome who died while on pilgrimage to Aran. This is not at all preposterous, as there was a point in history when Aran seemed to take on such huge importance as a place of pilgrimage as to be put on a par with Rome and Jerusalem.

It may refer to seven Irish pilgrims who also visited Rome in their lifetimes, and got the name Romani because of it. There was a native of Aran in recent memory who spent a part of his life in America before returning to live on Aran. From his return, he was always referred to as 'The American'.

It may refer to seven monks from the monastery who supported Rome. This perhaps is the most likely explanation. The Celtic-Roman tension came to the surface in 664 at the Synod of Whitby, in north-eastern England. This synod dealt with the dispute over the date of Easter. Underlying the dispute were other practices, for example, the monk's tonsure and the liturgy of baptism, where the Celtic practice differed from the Roman.

When a decision was made at this synod in favour of Rome, it caused a split in the Celtic Church. St Colman, the abbot of Lindisfarne further north, could not accept the decision and, with some fellow monks, packed his bags and came home to Ireland. From then on, each Celtic monastery had to grapple with the dilemma of being faithful to Rome or being faithful to the tradition of Colmcille.

The Romani movement, as it became known, continued to cause tension throughout Celtic monasteries at home and abroad up to the 12th century. In the 12th century, the Roman episcopalian model of church gained dominance over the Celtic monastic model. From then on the Celtic Church went into steep decline.

The VII ROMANI buried here are probably seven members of this monastic community who took the Roman view.

### *The High Crosses*

Unfortunately, all high crosses on Aran were smashed as part of the Cromwellian persecutions in the 17th century. The remains of two are to be found at Enda's monastery in Cill Éinne, and the remains of three are to be found here.

The first of these is the West Cross marking Leaba an Spioraid Naoimh beside St Breacán's Bed. It stood about two metres high. The second is the North Cross, situated a field's distance from the rest of the buildings. It is marked by a sign-post next to a stone wall. This cross was an astonishing four metres high, cut out of one piece of limestone. It would have made an imposing boundary marker and penitential station for pilgrims arriving at the monastery.

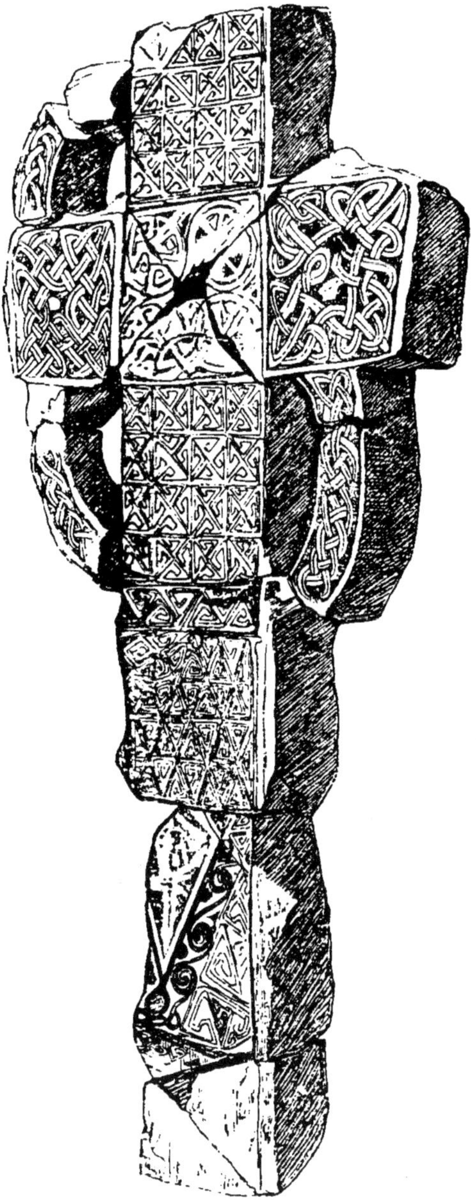

*South Cross at The Seven Churches*

*Artist: Margaret Stokes*

## The Evolution of the Celtic Cross

*In Megalithic times, stones were used to mark graves and to pinpoint energy alignments and cosmic concurrances. Fine examples of this are at Newgrange and Stonehenge.*

*When the Tuatha Dé Danann came to Ireland, they brought with them four sacred objects. One of these was the Lia Fáil (the Stone of Destiny). It was placed at the mythical centre of Ireland, the Hill of Tara. The stone shouted out when a future king of Ireland was in its presence. That stone is still at Tara today, linking us to pre-Celtic times.*

*The Celts used standing stones as markers — sometimes of a grave, sometimes of a sacred location such as a hilltop or energy point. Two examples are to be seen from Teampall An Cheathrair Álainn (see page 56).*

*The Celtic monks adapted the use of standing stones to their own purposes. They inscribed crosses on them and stood them in positions that marked the boundaries of their monasteries. Mainistir Chiaráin offers a good example of this (see page 43).*

*As the Celtic Church developed and the sculptors became masters of their craft, the cross-inscribed stone progressed to the more elaborate and artistically decorated Celtic Cross. There are the remains of three of these crosses at Na Seacht dTeampaill (see page 90). They are up to four metres high, and each one is different.*

The third cross, the South Cross, is more difficult to get to. It lies on the ledge above the level of the monastery, in the grounds of the round house. One can get to it by crossing the stile in the wall close to the VII ROMANI and turning right, going past the round house on your left. It is more easily accessible from the road and means walking through the front entrance of the round house (a private dwelling).

This cross is lying flat and is surrounded by a stone wall — the remains of St Breacán's chapel. The pieces of the cross have been fitted together and the whole lot cemented to a stone slab. This is unfortunate, as it means that only one side can be viewed. Across the way from the cross is a holy well — a rock cavity or natural bullán with a stone canopy.

Na Seacht dTeampaill is said to have been a mixed monastery. St Brigid was abbess of a similar mixed monastery in Kildare. Many Irish monasteries began as mixed monasteries and only changed to single sex as the Roman influence grew. Whether this was true of all the Aran monasteries we do not know. Looking through the annals of Irish history, it is clear that even where the monastic positions were for men only, many of these men, including abbots and bishops, were married or had concubines — and this was accepted practice.

There are no parts of buildings at Na Seacht dTeampaill that can be dated much earlier than the 12th or 13th centuries. Teampall an Phoill was built probably in the 16th century. All the domestic buildings were built around this time too.

This 16th century development suggests that the monastery may have been taken over by a European religious order. The Celtic monasteries had all but disappeared and any new development at this time raises questions. There are a few scraps of evidence that suggest the Canons Regular of St Augustine were here. The dormitory style accommodation, typical of these monasteries, lends credence to this theory.

Whatever the case, this and all the other monasteries on Inis Mór are now in ruins. A monastic presence that began in the late 5th century and lasted right through until at least the 16th century — 1100 years — finally came to an end. A unique expression of Christianity had been created on the rich cultural soil of Celtic Ireland.

In a way it was defeated by its own success. Success on the continent of Europe made it a threat to Rome. Success at home made it a threat to Britain. Success also brought wealth, political interference, and corruption — a deadly combination which inevitably brings collapse.

The beginning of the end was signalled as early as the 7th century by the Whitby decision. A death blow was struck in the 12th century when the Celtic abbots were disempowered and both authority and property were transferred to bishops and clergy. The Reformation and the dissolution of the monasteries by Henry VIII in the 1530s brought it to its final gasps. And the oppression which began under Cromwell in 1649 buried it.

While the Celtic Church died a death and its monastic structures lie in ruins, the spirituality which underlay it remains very much alive. That spirituality is in the process of being reclaimed by a movement that spans the Irish diaspora throughout the world. It is entirely possible that a new Celtic expression of church will emerge in our day and that the world will witness the resurrection of a tradition that had been in the grave for 350 years.

### *Eoghanacht Catholic Church*

Heading west from Na Seacht dTeampaill, you pass Eoghanacht Catholic church on your left. This is the most recent church to be built on Inis Mór. Opened in 1958 and dedicated to St Patrick and St Enda, the memory of its construction remains with the people of the island. The parish priest was the only person who owned a tractor. Each morning he would drive west through the island and pick up his meitheal oibre, his team of volunteers, for the day. In this way the church got built, just as most of the houses were built in those days — with the neighbourly labour of an meitheal oibre.

Eoghanacht church was built on a more ancient sacred site which had been used to erect funerary cairns and monuments to the dead. These were removed with the building of the church.

### *Two Clocháns*

Take the lane to the south off the road at Eoghanacht Catholic church. Take a right at a T-junction and then the next left. The lane leads to the top of the hill. At the top, you will see two clocháns or beehive huts in a field on the left. These clocháns are more or less intact, although it is clear they had collapsed and were rebuilt. These were hermit cells probably associated with the monastery below (see pages 77 and 78).

### *Next Stop America*

Back on the main road heading west, the road passes Eoghanacht National School and then takes a steep incline up Creig a' Chéirín. Having crossed the brow of the hill, one can see the end of the island, Bun Gabhla. Next stop America. A coast road to the north of Bun Gabhla offers an alternative route back, bringing you out at Na Seacht dTeampaill.

# Traditional Prayers When Doing the Rounds

In ainm an Athar, agus an Mhic agus an Spioraid Naoimh. Amen.

Ár nAthair atá ar neamh go naomhítear d'ainm. Go dtaga do ríocht. Go ndéantar do thoil ar an talamh mar a dhéantar ar neamh. Ár n-arán laethúil tabhair dúinn inniu agus maith dúinn ár bhfiacha mar a mhaithimidne dár bhféichiúna féin; agus ná lig sinn i gcathú, ach saor sinn ó olc. Amen.

Sé do bheatha a Mhuire, atá lán de ghrásta; tá an Tiarna leat, is beannaithe thú idir mná agus is beannaithe toradh do bhroinne, Íosa. A NaomhMhuire, a mháthair Dé, guigh orainn na peacaigh, anois agus ar uair ár mbáis. Amen.

Glóir don Athair, don Mhac agus don Spiorad Naomh. Mar a bhí ar dtús, mar atá anois, agus mar a bhéas go brách, le saol na saol. Amen.

Creidim i nDia, an tAthair uilechumhachtach, cruthaitheoir neimhe agus talún; agus in Íosa Críost, a aon mhacsan, ár dTiarna, a gabhadh ón Spiorad Naomh, a rugadh ó Mhuire Ógh; a d'fhulaing páis faoi Phontius Píoláit, a céasadh ar chrois, a fuair bás agus a adhlacadh; a chuaigh síos go hifreann, a d'éirigh an treas lá ó mhairbh; a chuaigh suas ar neamh; atá ina shuí ar dheis Dé, an tAthair uile-chumhachtach; as sin tiocfaidh sé chun breithiúnas a thabhairt ar bheo agus ar mhairbh. Creidim sa Spiorad Naomh, sa NaomhEaglais Chaitliceach, i gcomaoin na naomh; i maithiúnas na bpeacaí, in aiséirí na colainne, agus sa bheatha shíoraí. Amen.

*English translation on next page*

In the name of the Father, and of the Son, and of the Holy Spirit. Amen.

Our Father, who art in heaven, hallowed be thy name, thy kingdom come, thy will be done on earth as it is in heaven. Give us this day our daily bread and forgive us our trespasses, as we forgive those who trespass against us, and lead us not into temptation, but deliver us from evil. Amen.

Hail Mary, full of grace, the Lord is with thee. Blessed art thou among women, and blessed is the fruit of thy womb, Jesus. Holy Mary, mother of God, pray for us sinners, now and at the hour of our death. Amen.

Glory be to the Father, and to the Son and to the Holy Spirit. As it was in the beginning, is now and ever shall be, world without end. Amen.

I believe in God, the Father Almighty, creator of heaven and earth. And in Jesus Christ, his only Son, Our Lord, who was conceived of the Holy Spirit, born of the virgin Mary, suffered under Pontius Pilate, was crucified, died and was buried. He descended into hell. The third day He arose again from the dead and ascended into heaven where He is seated at the right hand of God, the Father Almighty. From there He shall come to judge the living and the dead. I believe in the Holy Spirit, the holy catholic church, the communion of saints, the forgiveness of sins, the resurrection of the body and life everlasting. Amen.

# Further Reading

## Aran Islands

*Oileáin Árann, a companion to the map of the Aran Islands,* **Tim Robinson**, Folding Landscapes, Roundstone, Co. Galway, Ireland, 1996. (The map itself is by the same author & publisher).
*Stones of Aran — Pilgrimage,* **Tim Robinson**, The Lilliput Press/Wolfhound Press, Dublin, 1986.
*Stones of Aran — Labyrinth,* **Tim Robinson**, The Lilliput Press, Dublin, 1995.
*An Aran Reader,* edited by **Breandán and Ruairí Ó hEithir**, The Lilliput Press, Dublin, 1991.
*Oileáin Árann - Stair na n-Oileán anuas go dtí 1922,* **Antoine Powell**, Wolfhound Press, Dublin.
*The Aran Islands,* **J.M. Synge**, first published 1907, reprinted, Oxford University Press, Oxford, 1962.
*Oileáin Árann,* **Leo Daly**, Albertine Kennedy, Swinford, Co. Mayo 1975, and Hayden House Publications, Mullingar, 1996.
*Mementos of Mortality, the Cenotaphs and Funerary Cairns of Árainn,* **Tim Robinson**, Folding Landscapes, Roundstone, Co. Galway, Ireland, 1991.
*The Book of Aran, The Aran Islands, Co. Galway* edited by **John Waddell, J.W.O'Connell** and **Anne Korff.** Published by Tír Eolas, Newtownlynch, Kinvara, co. Galway. 1994.

## Irish Mythology

*The Encyclopaedia of Celtic Wisdom,* **Caitlín and John Matthews**, Element Books, Dorset, UK, 1994.
*Over Nine Waves, a Book of Irish Legends,* **Marie Heaney**, Faber and Faber, London, 1994.
*A Guide to Irish Mythology,* **Daragh Smyth**, Irish Academic Press, Dublin, 1988.
*Mythic Ireland,* **Michael Dames**, Thames and Hudson, London, 1992.
*Myths and Legends of the Celtic Race,* **T W Rolleston**, Constable, London, 1992.
*Myth, Legend & Romance, an Encyclopaedia of the Irish Folk Tradition,* **Dr Daithí O hÓgain**, Prentice Hall Press, New York, 1991.
*Celtic Gods, Celtic Goddesses,* **R.J. Stewart**, Blandford, an imprint of Cassell, London, 1990.

## Celtic Church — Monasticism

*Irish Monasticism,* **John Ryan SJ**, Colour Books, Dublin, 1931.
*Celtic Monasticism,* **Kathleen Hughes and Ann Hamlin**, The Seabury Press, New York, 1981; originally published as: The Modern Traveller to the Early Irish Church, 1977.
*How the Irish Saved Civilization,* **Thomas Cahill**, Hodder and Stoughton, London, 1995.

***Early Celtic Christianity*, Brendan Lehane**, Barnes and Noble/Viking Books, USA, 1968.
***Isle of the Saints*, Lisa M. Bitel**, Cornell University Press, Ithaca, New York,1990.
***The Celtic Alternative*, Shirley Toulson**, Rider, London, 1987.

## Celtic Spirituality

***Anam Cara, Spiritual Wisdom from the Celtic World*, John O'Donohue**, Bantam Press, a division of Transworld Publishers, London, 1997.
***The Celtic Way of Prayer*, Esther De Waal**, Hodder and Stoughton, London, 1996.
***The Saints of Ireland*, Mary Ryan D'Arcy**, Irish American Cultural Institute, St. Paul, Minnesota, 1974.
***Wisdom of the Celtic Saints*, Edward C. Sellner**, Ave Maria Press, Notre Dame, Indiana, 1993.
***Living Between Worlds — Place and Journey in Celtic Spirituality*, Philip Sheldrake**, Darton, Longman and Todd, London, 1995.
***A World Made Whole — Rediscovering the Celtic Tradtion*, Esther De Waal**, Fount Paperbacks, London, 1991.
***Where Three Streams Meet: Celtic Spirituality*, Seán Ó Duinn OSB**, Columba Press, Dublin 2000.
***The Celtic Soul Friend, A Trusted Guide for Today*, Edward C. Sellner**, Ave Maria Press, Notre Dame, Indiana, 2002.
***Kindling the Celtic Spirit, Ancient Traditions to Illumine Your Life Throughout the Seasons*, Mara Freeman**, Harper San Francisco, 2001.
*Ár bPaidreacha DÚchais*, collected and edited by **Diarmuid Ó Laoghaire, S.J.** Foilseacháin Ábhair Spioradálta, Dublin. 1975.

## Other

***The Serpent and the Goddess*, Mary Condren**, Harper and Row, San Francisco, 1989.
***Celtic Threads: Exploring the Wisdom of Our Heritage***, edited by **Padraigín Clancy.** Veritas Publications, Dublin. 1999.

## Web Sites

**<www.visitaranislands.com>**
Website of Comharchumann Forbartha Árann, the Inis Mór Community Co-operative.
**<www.discoveryprogramme.ie>**
Website of the Irish Government's archaeological programme which includes the excavations at Dún Aonghusa.
**<www.aislingmagazine.com>**
Website of a magazine published on Inis Mór by Dara Ó Maoildhia and Tess Harper. Contains articles on Celtic heritage and spirituality.
**<www.iolfree.ie/~daramolloy>**
Website of Dara Ó Maoildhia, the author of this book.

# Travel Information

**TO IRELAND**

**By Plane**

Flights to Dublin Airport and Shannon Airport from Europe and the U.S.

**By Boat**

Sailings to Dublin from Liverpool and Holyhead in UK.

Sailings to Rosslare from Fishguard and Pembroke in UK and from Cherbourg, and Le Havre in France.

Sailings to Cork from Swansea, Le Havre, and Roscoff.

**TO GALWAY CITY**

From **Dublin City** by **bus**: directly from the airport to Galway via Nestor Bus Company, City Link Bus Company, or Bus Eireann. No need to book. These buses also leave from Dublin city centre.

From **Dublin City** by **train**: train departs from Heuston Station. Bus to station from O'Connell Bridge in city centre.

From **Dublin Airport** by **plane**: book with Aer Árann <www.aerarann.ie>.

From **Rosslare**: by bus or train first to Dublin and then to Galway, or by bus via Limerick.

From **Cork**: by bus via Limerick.

**TO INIS MÓR FROM GALWAY**

**By boat from Rossaveel**: Rossaveel is 23 miles NW of Galway city.

**— to Rossaveel by car**: travel the coast road from Galway city via Salthill and Spiddal. Allow 75 minutes.

**— to Rossaveel by bus**: two ferry companies offer a bus service from Galway city to connect with their boat sailings. Both ferry companies, Inis Mór Ferries and Island Ferries, have offices located in Forster Street close to the Bus and Rail Station at the foot of Eyre Square. Buses leave from closeby.

**Ferry Sailings**: Sailings in winter are twice daily. First sailing 10.30 am. Sailings in summer are every 2-3 hours throughout the day. Ferries sail seven days a week throughout the year. The boats are modern and fast. Sailing time: 45 minutes.

**By Plane from Inverin**: Aer Árann operates a daily service to the islands. The airstrip at Inverin is 20 miles from Galway city on the road to Rossaveel.

**Sailings from Doolin and Galway city**: A cargo vessel departs daily in the summer from Galway Docks and carries passengers. The sailing takes two hours. A small passenger ferry departs daily in the summer from Doolin, Co. Clare and visits all three islands. For either of these contact: O'Brien Shipping.

**Phone Numbers:**

*Inis Mór Ferries* +353-(0)91-566535 / 534553 / 595036

*Island Ferries* +353-(0)91-561767 / 572050

*Aer Árann* +353-(0)91-593034 / 593054

*O'Brien Shipping* +353-(0)91-567676; Doolin: +353-(0)65-7074455

*Ireland West Tourism* +353-(0)91-563081; +353-(0)99-61263

# Accommodation

**Guest Houses** — The following guest houses / B.&B.s serve evening meals.

*Pier House,* Kilronan. Tel. +353-(0)99-61416 / 61417.

*Dormer House,* Kilronan. Tel. +353-(0)99-61125.

*Ard Éinne,* Killeany, two miles from Kilronan. Tel. +353-(0)99-61126.

*Man of Aran Cottages,* Kilmurvey, four miles Kilronan. Tel. +353-(0)99-61301.

*Kilmurvey House,* Kilmurvey, four miles from Kilronan. Tel. +353-(0)99-61218.

*Mainistir House Hostel,* Mainistir, 1 mile from Kilronan. Tel. +353-(0)99-61169.

*Tí Fitz,* Killeany, 1 mile from Kilronan. Tel. +353-(0)99-61213.

**B.&B.s** — there are plenty of B.&B.s on Inis Mór and they can be booked through Ireland West Tourism, tel. +353-(0)91-563081 or +353-(0)99-61263.

**Hostels** — The main hostels are:

*Mainistir House,* tel. +353-(0)99-61169. One mile outside Kilronan. 100 beds. Serves breakfast and evening meals.

*Kilronan Hostel,* tel. +353-(0)99-61255. In Kilronan. 50 beds.

*Killeany Lodge Pilgrim Hostel,* tel. +353-(0)99-61393 / 61245. One and a half miles outside Kilronan. 24 beds including private rooms. Available for exclusive booking by groups. Facilities for workshops and courses.

**Dining Out** — during the day there are numerous places where one can take a snack with soup and sandwiches or chips. In the evening, the main restaurants open are:

*Fisherman Restaurant,* in main village of Kilronan.

*Pier House Restaurant,* in main village of Kilronan.

*Mainistir House,* 1 mile outside Kilronan village.

*Teach Nan Phaidí,* in village of Kilmurvey.

*Man of Aran Cottages Restaurant,* outside village of Kilmurvey.

*Tí Fitz,* in Killeany, 1 mile from Kilronan.

**Transport on Inis Mór**

**Mini-buses:** these are the main form of motorised transport for visitors to the island. They are available at the pier at boat arrival times, and can also be hired privately at any time.

**Pony and Trap:** a pony and trap can be hired from Kilronan village.

**Bicycles:** there are a number of bicycle hire outlets in Kilronan village.

**Shops** — There is one main supermarket in Kilronan village. Many small craft shops are to be found in Kilronan and Kilmurvey.

**Rented Accommodation** — contact Ireland West Tourism (see phone numbers above).

**Tour and Pilgrim Guide** — contact Dara Ó Maoildhia, at +353-(0)99-61245.

# Glossary

Aill - cliff
Altóir - altar
Aingeal - angel
Bád - boat
Bóithrín - lane or narrow road
Bóthar - road
Bullán - a hollowed out stone
Caoineadh - keening, crying of women in grief
Carraig - rock
Caiseal - cashel, stone defence wall
Cill - cell or chapel
Cloch - stone
Clochán - beehive stone hut
Coláiste - college
Cosán - footpath
Creig - flat slab of rock
Crois - cross
Dabhach - casket, barrel or container
Díseart - desert place
Drúcht - dew
Dúchas - native heritage
Dúirling - stone beach
Dún - fort
Fir Bolg - literally 'stomach men'
Garraí - Garden
Geis - a spell or enchantment
Gleann - valley
Gort - field
Halla - hall
Inis - island
Iomair - bowl or container
Leaba - bed, normally meant as burial place
Leacht - stone slab
Leachtaí cuimhneacháin - stone memorials
Loch - lake
Mac - son, as in Mac Duach
Mainistir - monastery
Meitheal oibre - group gathered for mutual aid
Naomh - saint
Ó - from, as in Ó'Donoghue
Sídhe - fairies, people who live underground
Teach - house
Teaghlach - household
Teampall - church, literally a temple
Tír na nÓg - country of the young
Tobar - well
Turas deiseal - prayer round, journey to the right
Turlough - lake that dries up
Tuatha Dé Danaan - country people of goddess Danu
Reilig - graveyard

# Index